SACRED
JOURNEY

SACRED JOURNEY

LIVING PURPOSEFULLY AND DYING GRACEFULLY

SWAMI RAMA

Himalayan Institute Hospital Trust
Swami Rama Nagar, P.O. Doiwala
Distt. Dehradun 248140, Uttaranchal, India

Acknowledgments

We would like to express our appreciation to Mr. Richard Kenyon for compiling the text from its various sources, to Dr. Barbara Bova for editing, and to Connie Gage for designing the cover. And to Wesley Van Linda we would like to express our gratitude for the many services rendered to make this venture possible.

© 2002 by the Himalayan Institute Hospital Trust

First USA edition, 2002
Printed in the United States of America
ISBN 8-188157-00-7
Library of Congress Control Number: 2002105138

Published by:

Himalayan Institute Hospital Trust
Swami Rama Nagar, P.O. Doiwala
Distt. Dehradun 248140, Uttaranchal, India
Tel: 91-135-412068, Fax: 91-135-412008
hihtsrc@sancharnet.in; www.hihtindia.org

Distributed by:
Lotus Press, P.O. Box 325
Twin Lakes, WI 53181
www.lotuspress.com
lotuspress@lotuspress.com
800-824-6396

Contents

Introduction

This book is about the relationship between life and death, and the "how and why" of organizing one's life in a way that leads to expansion and growth, and that is helpful in preparing for the transition we call death.

Modern civilization is a marvel of technological achievement, material wealth, and communications systems that have shrunk the globe. In spite of all the wealth and ease of modern life, people are not content. They are not happy because of their attitude toward the objects of the world and toward their relationships with others. Throughout their lives they uphold the notion that they must have more and more possessions. They have a similar notion about relationships and maintain that something is to be received from a relationship rather than given. Instead of simply enjoying the objects and people in their lives, they cling to them, own them, and fear losing them.

Over the course of a lifetime of needing, having, and clinging, the fear of death grows and hovers, creating a spiral of more need, greater fear, and inescapable pain. In this way life cannot be lived effectively and is merely squandered. Death is feared, denied, and pushed as far away from consciousness as possible instead of being accepted as a natural and inevi-

table part of human experience. Thus, no one is prepared for death.

This fear of death is the reason for the insatiable
need for more things, ever new relationsips, material
comforts, endless entertainment, and the excessive use
of alcohol and drugs. All of these keep the reality of
death in the distance. They are the tools of denial.
Unfortunately, they are not useful tools.

To understand death, a person must try to understand the purpose of life and the relationship between life and death. The two are partners, each pro-
viding a context for the other. Death is not a period,
but merely a pause on a long journey. When life and
death are accepted as having real meaning and purpose, and death is understood and accepted as part
of the human journey, then the fear of death disappears and life can be lived fully.

This book is about the relationship between life
and death, and the "how and why" of organizing
one's life in a way that leads to expansion and growth,
and that is helpful in preparing for the transition we
call death.

The path described in this book is derived largely
from the ancient Indian scriptures known as the
Upanishads, the great scriptures that comprise the
latter part of the Vedas, the oldest spiritual revelations in the history of humankind.

There are four Vedas—Rik, Yajus, Sama, and
Atharva—and each is divided into two general sections. The first section of each is made up of hymns,
rules of conduct, and instructions on the performance
of rites and sacraments. The metaphysical section attached to each deals with the knowledge of the absolute Reality. These later sections are the Upanishads.

Tradition counts one hundred eight Upanishads,
although there are closer to two hundred Upanishads

in existence. Of these, ten expound the Vedantic philosophy. They are recognized as revealed texts, the wisdom that came to seers in the most purified and transcendental state known as *samadhi*. The seers passed them on to disciples who reverentially preserved them from one generation to the next.

The word Upanishad means *to sit down near* — to sit at the feet of a master and listen to the narration of these profound and often esoteric and symbolic scriptures.

Another interpretation is that the word Upanishad comes from the Sanskrit verb *sad*, which means to destroy, loosen, or guide. Upanishad is that which destroys the ignorance that binds a human being to that which is transitory. Upanishad helps to loosen one's attachment to the material world and the physical, perishable self, giving guidance for attainment of the final goal.

These scriptures teach that human life has a purpose and a meaning. Innately all human beings know this, even though they may argue and create philosophies that maintain that life is aimless, just an accidental occurrence in a limitless universe. In one way or another everyone strives for happiness, calmness, and peace of heart and mind.

The Upanishads are maps that show the path of liberation and the meaning of life and death. That path is made clear by a central theme that runs through these scriptures: everything is essentially One.

One of the outstanding and exceptional teachings in the Upanishads is that the phenomenal universe is a manifestation rather than a creation. One absolute Reality has been manifested into many. This is different from the western idea of a creator who is separate from the creation. Duality is completely discarded in the teachings of the Upanishads. *Eko'ham*

buhu syam. There is only One, here, there, and everywhere. The One is *Brahman,* the Upanishadic term
for the Reality, or pure consciousness. "Brahman is
real," state the Upanishads, "and the transitory objects of the world are unreal." Everything other than
Brahman is illusory. Brahman is the source of life, light,
and existence. The purpose of life is to realize this truth.

The tendency of most people is to look exter-
nally to the objects of the world for happiness. The
Upanishads, on the other hand, tell us that happiness is not to be found in the things of the world. Those
things, including relationships, are fleeting, and what
is fleeting cannot provide lasting peace or joy.

The Upanishads tell us to look within to find
what is everlasting. "Man looks toward what is without, and sees not what is within," say the Upanishads.
"Rare is he who, longing for immortality, shuts his
eyes to what is without and beholds the Self. Fools
follow the desires of the flesh and fall into the snare
of all encompassing death, but the wise, knowing the
Self as eternal, seek not the things that pass away."

How similar this is to what St. Paul wrote to the
Corinthians when he reminded them that everything
in life is for spiritual growth. "All things are for your
sakes," he said. "Use them wisely. Life is brief.

"...though your outward man perish, yet the
inward man is renewed day by day for the things
which are seen are temporal, but things which are
not seen are eternal."

Jesus likewise guided his disciples in the Sermon
on the Mount:

"Lay not up for yourselves treasures upon earth,
where moth and rust do corrupt, and where thieves
break through and steal. But lay up for yourselves
treasures in heaven, where neither moth nor rust cor-

rupts, and where thieves do not break through nor steal.

"For where your treasure is, there will your heart be also."

Life's purpose is to know the distinction between what is outside and fleeting, and what is inside and eternal, and to discover through practice and experience the infinite value of one to the other. Once this distinction is realized life takes on a joyful meaning and the fear of death evaporates.

The Upanishads are also known as the Vedanta, or the end of the Vedas, and as such they express the highest purpose, which is to attain the supreme knowledge that frees the individuated soul from bondage.

This book is the outcome of a lecture series delivered at Congresses at Chicago and Honesdale, Pennsylvania, USA. Minor corrections have been made here and there.

Swami Rama
Jolly Grant, Dehradun, U.P., India
November, 1995

Chapter One

Kathopanishad

The Upanishad examined in this book is the Kathopanishad, a scripture that unveils the mystery of death and the meaning of life.

An old story is told about the beginning of time. The universe was in the process of being created and not everything was yet in order or fully functioning. Before the universe could be totally engaged, the Creator had one final task to complete. To help him complete this task the Lord summoned an angel.

The angel came. The Creator told the angel that he, the Lord, had one last job to do in the making of the universe.

"I saved the best for last," the Creator told the angel. "I have here the real meaning of human life, the treasure of life, the purpose and goal of all this that I have created.

"Because this treasure is valuable beyond description," the Creator continued, "I want you to hide it. Hide this treasure so well that human beings will know its value to be immeasurable."

"I will do so, Lord," said the angel. "I will hide the treasure of life on the highest mountain top."

"The treasure will be too easy to find there," said the Creator.

"Then," said the angel, "I will hide the treasure

in the great desert wilderness. Surely, the treasure will not be easily found there."

"No, too easy."

"In the vast reaches of the universe?" asked the angel. "That would make a difficult search."

"No," the Creator said pondering. Then his face showed a flash of inspiration. "I know. I have the place. Hide the treasure of life within the human being. He will look there last and know how precious this treasure is. Yes, hide the treasure there."

This treasure and the search for it are the subjects of the Upanishads. Given the nature of human beings, that treasure was indeed well hidden. As the Lord said in the story above, the last place human beings will look for the ultimate Reality is within themselves. They will look to all the diverse objects of the world for meaning, and each time, with each well-meant effort, come away with nothing worth having. In this way a perpetual cycle of births and deaths is created. They spend life running after things that are only temporal and when death comes they are empty handed, with just an invitation to do it over again.

The Upanishads say the ignorant person keeps accepting that invitation, but the wise person sees the futility in the endless pattern of death and rebirth, and looks within for that which is eternal.

According to the Upanishads, that which we seek within is called *Atman,* the pure Self, our real identity, that, as the Bible says, is in the image and likeness of God. The real Self is not recognizable by the senses or the mind. It is the hidden treasure within the soul, and dwells in the innermost chamber of the heart. It is very subtle, unfathomable, and eternal. It existed at the beginning of creation, exists now, and will continue to exist in the future.

The phenomenal universe, as the Upanishads explain repeatedly, is impermanent and constantly changing, evolving, growing, decaying, and dying. It goes on endlessly this way — coming, going, dying. That is its nature. Anyone who becomes attached to the phenomenal world with all of its changing forms is sure to come to grief in the end. Yet the phenomenal world plays a role in bringing a person to the realm of the immortal. The pain and fear of death that are natural to the material world are meant to guide a person toward wisdom. A time comes when the individual realizes that there must be more to existence than this. Then he or she begins to seriously look for an alternative as the ultimate purpose of life.

The Upanishad examined in this book is the Kathopanishad, a scripture that unveils the mystery of death and the meaning of life. Of all the Upanishads, Kathopanishad is the most lucid and accessible on the knowledge of Atman here and hereafter. It clearly defines the alternatives confronting humanity concerning the purpose of life and the ultimate choices that have to be made.

This Upanishad is a beautiful, poetic explanation of the mystery of life and death, the law of karma, and how to attain liberation from grief and distress. It is composed in one hundred nineteen mantras and constructed around a dialogue between a spiritually minded young man named Nachiketa on one hand and Yama, the king of death on the other. Yama, unlike portrayals in Greek or Roman mythology of the king of death, is not something dreadful. He was the first man born on the earth to die and was a self realized master. In this scripture, Yama may be compared to the highest discriminating intelligence of the human being, while Nachiketa represents the lower mind, albeit with strength and courage.

The dialogue between the two reveals the character of a dedicated but yet unrealized spiritual seeker. Nachiketa is someone we can understand as well as admire. Though he has many doubts, his faith is indisputable. Above all he harbors a deep desire for the highest knowledge and ultimate happiness.

Nachiketa is tested by Yama to determine how strong his desire for truth is. Is it stronger than the attractions to the things of desire in the world? Yes. Nachiketa renounces everything for the sake of Self-realization. Above all else he wants to know Atman, the real Self.

In his faith Nachiketa knows that all the pleasures, even the highest joys of life, do not continue forever. They pass away, leaving pain in their wake. No matter where one goes, or what one does, as long as worldly desires are present there can be no real peace. It doesn't matter whether a person lives totally in the world, surrounded by and fully partaking of the world's pleasures, or in the wilderness apart from all enticements. Whenever there are desires for worldly things there will be discontent.

Death is no more an escape from all these desires than is the barren desert wilderness. People cling to their desires till death and drag them all back with them again to the worldly plane where they can be fulfilled.

It is only in practical daily life that people can deal with desires and attain self-control over the senses and thoughts that drive the desires. People must learn to rise above desires and see their limited value. Only when they rise above desires and gain mastery over their senses and thoughts will they begin to realize real joy. They will see that as they let go of their attachments to worldly things, including their own material bodies, they will begin to experience a sense of peace of immeasurably greater value than any wealth or comfort material existence could ever offer. Nachiketa understood this innately. You might say his conscience was directing him, and he had the courage to follow his conscience instead of tracing the well-worn steps of so many others who chose the path of material pursuits.

The path described by Yama in the Kathopanishad is the path of yoga, whose aim is the spiritual union between the individual soul and the supreme Self of all.

Chapter Two

Nachiketa's Choice

The journey to the discovery of the real self is the goal or the purpose of life.

Nachiketa's story in the Kathopanishad begins when his wealthy father, Vajashravas, is to perform a special sacrifice. The sacrifice required Vajashravas to give all his wealth, all his possessions, and distribute them to the great seers and Brahmins. It was a rare sacrifice performed only by the most highly advanced aspirants. One who could give up all transitory things would have the knowledge of Brahman, the knowledge of Reality.

The story is not unlike the New Testament meeting of Jesus with the rich, young ruler who asks what it will take to have eternal life. After the rich man assures Jesus that he has obeyed the commandments against murder, stealing, adultery, and lying all his life, and has honored his mother and father, and loved his neighbor, Jesus gives him a single instruction. He tells the rich man he must give away all that he has to the poor, and come with him.

The rich man cannot. Although virtuous in every respect, he is too attached to his worldly possessions and wealth. The scriptures tell us that the rich man went away sorrowful.

Nachiketa's father also could not part with his wealth, despite the assurance that the knowledge of Brahman would follow the sacrifice.

The Kathopanishad tells us he brought cows for giving away as part of the sacrifice, but only those cows that were old, dry, blind, diseased, and of little or no use to anybody. Vajashravas kept the good cows for himself.

Nachiketa saw the old and useless cows his father brought for the sacrifice and knew such an unworthy gift would bring misery to his father. Eager to help his father, Nachiketa reminded his father that as his son he was also his property and should be included in the sacrifice for distribution.

"Father, to whom will you give me?" asked Nachiketa.

Vajashravas, haunted by the knowledge of his halfhearted sacrifice, focused his negative emotion on his son and chose to interpret Nachiketa's offer as impudence.

Three times Nachiketa asked his father to whom he would be given. After the third time, Vajashravas angrily retorted. "You I shall give to the Ruler of Death, Yama."

Nachiketa, with a pure heart and an abundance of faith, cheerfully took his father at his word.

"There is nothing in death," said Nachiketa. "All beings flourish like grain and die again. Now I shall be the first one to discover truth and reveal the mystery of death."

When Nachiketa went to Yama's abode, the Ruler of Death was not at home. Three nights passed before Yama returned. To make amends for not being there to welcome his guest, Yama gave Nachiketa three boons, one for each night he had waited alone without proper hospitality.

Nachiketa's first boon, demonstrating again the respect he had for his father, asked Yama to soothe Vajashravas' heart, to allay his father's anger, and to remove any worry Vajashravas might have because Nachiketa was now away from home.

Yama granted the wish and said, "Oh, Nachiketa, your father will happily recognize you and treat you with the greatest love and kindness. "

For his second boon, Nachiketa asked Yama to show him the fire sacrifice and all the rituals and ceremonies that went with it.

"In heaven," said Nachiketa in his request for the second boon, "there is neither fear nor death, neither age nor decay, neither hunger nor thirst, neither pain nor suffering. There is perpetual bliss. Ruler of Death, you alone know how, by performing sacrifice, mortals can attain this blissful heaven. This is my second boon that I ask. I want to know the nature of the sacrifice which leads a mortal to heaven."

Yama granted it, and taught Nachiketa the fire sacrifice. Yama then told Nachiketa to choose his third boon. After going within himself and quieting himself, Nachiketa said to Yama:

"There is a belief that after a man departs from the world he is gone forever. There is another viewpoint that he is born again, that even after death man does not die in the real sense but remains on a subtle plane with his subtle body, and only the outer physical garment is discarded; and that is called death. There is yet another belief that one who dies, lives. Which of these is true? What exists after death? Explain it to me. This is my third request—the truth relating to the mystery of death."

Yama did not want to explain the mystery of death to Nachiketa without testing the eagerness and sincerity of his young disciple. Yama told Nachiketa that even the gods had difficulty understanding this mystery.

"It is very difficult for anyone to grasp," said Yama. "Ask any other boon and I shall grant it to you with great pleasure."

Nachiketa was steadfast. He told Yama that even though the gods were once puzzled by the mystery of death, and even though the subject was difficult to understand, there was no better teacher than Yama to explain it.

"Oh King of Death," said Nachiketa, "I shall not make any other request. There is no boon equal to this and I must know the secret."

Yama tried another route and tested Nachiketa with the temptations all human beings face, the choice between God and mammon, between passing material pleasures and eternal joy, between illusion and reality.

Yama offered Nachiketa a life span of as many years as he might wish, with all the pleasures there are in heaven. Yama said he would grant Nachiketa children, grandchildren, and great grandchildren, fine horses and elephants, gold, jewels, and rare gems. He said he would give Nachiketa the kingdom of earth to rule. He did not want to grant the third boon requested by Nachiketa.

"Take all of this wealth and power instead of the third boon that is asked for," said Yama to Nachiketa. "I shall fulfill all your desires," Yama continued, "except this, for it is the greatest secret of life. All the maidens in the celestial regions, such as cannot be had by ordinary mortals, shall be yours if you want them. Do not ask me that question again. I do not wish to divulge the secret of life and death."

Nachiketa then showed the depth of his faith

and resolve to know the purpose of life and the relationship between life and death. He was not interested in the temptations Yama offered him. He did not hesitate in answering Yama. He told the Ruler of Death.

"What shall I do with all these transitory and perishable objects? Everything that is perceived by the senses is momentary, and life on this plane is subject to change by death and decay. Even life in heaven is not worth living without acquiring the knowledge of liberation. All your dancing maidens and worldly attractions are merely sensual pleasures. Oh King of Death, keep them with you. No one can acquire happiness by worldly wealth. All the material enjoyments of this world and even heavenly life are subject to change. After knowing the fleeting nature of this world, who will long for mere longevity? I don't care to live for a thousand years. What shall I do with such a long life if I cannot acquire the highest wisdom and attain the supreme knowledge?"

When Yama saw the clarity and determination of Nachiketa, he gladly offered to grant the third boon.

Now the Kathopanishad begins in earnest to reveal the secret of immortality, the meaning of death and life.

Worldly, transitory life, with all of its charms, is not the purpose of human existence. The world is full of objects and temptations. People want them, choose them, and organize their lives around getting them, lifetime after lifetime.

Today a person develops a pattern of identifying with the world, with its objects, and with the emotions that go with having those objects or with the possibility of losing them. He begins to think that joy will come with having glamorous possessions, a new car, a new suit, or a new spouse. With each new acquisition there is a flash of satisfaction followed by a prolonged sense of dissatisfaction.

A person identifies with the emotions that go with the objects and relationships. He thinks he loves someone, that he must have her to be happy. When he has her, so often the relationship settles into something else that is not very loving. He may hurt the person he said he needed. Then he says he is sorry. A month passes and he does the same hurtful thing again. Finally, they separate. So he finds another person he thinks he needs for his happiness, and the process begins all over again.

There are many variations of this theme. The point is that a human being becomes attached to things and relationships, and the thoughts and emotions attendant to the attachments. That creates suffering because none of those things or relationships lasts. Nonetheless, human beings keep trying to find peace in this way, lifetime after lifetime.

"Those who are dwelling in the darkness of ignorance and are deluded by wealth and possessions are like children playing with toys," says Yama to Nachiketa. "Such foolish children are caught in the snares of death and come again and again under my sway. They remain in the snares of death. They cannot get beyond the limits of the dark realm. They travel back and forth."

Fortunately, this condition is not permanent. Eventually a time comes when the desire for all of those objects—what the nineteenth century Bengali saint Ramakrishna repeatedly referred to as lust and greed—begins to appear as empty and pointless.

Growth and expansion are the nature of the soul, so inevitably what happens is: a person comes to recognize the pattern that behind every pleasure is pain, behind every expectation is disappointment, and following every fulfilled desire is yet another desire. For all the world's charms, the bottom line and the sum of it all adds up to an inordinate amount of suffering, loneliness, and emptiness.

That arithmetic is instructive. The bottom line awakens the human soul. Suffering teaches and trains a person in the necessary art of discrimination.

The Kathopanishad outlines a pure, unequivocal choice. Yama tells Nachiketa that there are two alternative paths before us in the world. One is good and the other is pleasant. One, though difficult, leads to the knowledge of the highest Truth. The other, though appearing very pleasant, is ephemeral and when an apparently pleasurable experience passes, as it inevitably will, there is pain. The wise choose that which is good, and the ignorant rely on that which is pleasant.

That is the nature of life. The purpose of life is to grow, expand, and completely realize one's own true identity. If the path toward that goal is not taken, then the world will bring one around toward it. Blow after blow, one misfortune will follow another, one disappointment, then another, until the person begins to understand. The choice between good and pleasant becomes clear.

The theme of Kathopanishad is that the treasure of human life, the real Self, is to be found within. Within is immortality. Within is where Atman or Reality resides. The journey to the discovery of the real Self is the goal or the purpose of life. One who has realized one's own real Self can then realize the cosmic Self who encompasses the entire universe.

The dualists believe that the individual, the universe, and the cosmic Self are entirely separate units, having their independent existence. According to this belief, by knowing one's own Self one acquires only a partial knowledge. A wide gulf separates this school of thought from Vedanta. The most valuable and elevating contribution of Vedantic literature is that the Self, or God, is not separate or far away from us, but dwells within the inner chamber of our being. This is the central tenet in the philosophy of Vedanta.

Chapter Three

The Treasure

It is concealed within the heart of all beings.

The treasure according to Vedanta is Atman, the Self or absolute Reality, that exists within all individuals. In the language of the Bible, Atman is the image of God, that which is identical to Brahman, pure consciousness, ultimate Reality, or however else we attempt to express with words that which is indescribable. Atman and Brahman are one, just as Jesus said, "I and my Father are one."

"Be perfect as your Father in heaven is perfect," Jesus told his disciples. Know your identity with God. You are the same but have forgotten it, is the message. So remember. Do that essential work of remembering, of getting the clutter removed so you can remember.

Let's define some terms here, with the understanding that words are subject to limitations, whereas what we are talking about is beyond words and intellect. As the book of Tao says, the Tao that can be spoken of is not the real Tao. So also the Buddha instructed his disciples not to think or argue about God. Because of this instruction, Buddha and Buddhism are misunderstood as being atheistic. What the Buddha meant was that God, or pure consciousness, is beyond the limited mind, beyond the intellect. As soon as God is considered and defined by the limited mind, God becomes limited. So Buddha told his disciples to concentrate on removing the barriers that separated them from the true Self. When that is done, then whatever we call the ultimate Truth reveals itself.

With that said, the Vedantins nonetheless made a valiant effort to give these ideas perspective. Brahman is absolute existence, knowledge and bliss, the summum bonum of the life of all creatures. According to Vedantic terminology, Brahman is real and all else is unreal. That which is not subject to death, decay, and decomposition is real, and that which changes is temporal and unreal. The universe is not real. It cannot be real if it is only temporary. Another way of saying this is that the universe is not nonexistent, but it is not real in the same sense as Brahman.

When you dream, for the extent of the dream, the world that is created within the dream and the people and events in it are real. When you wake up that reality disappears. The worldly plane of the universe is considered by Vedantins to be as a dream. It is real within its own context, and it has purpose. Vedantins call it maya, an illusion. It is neither absolutely real, nor absolutely nonexistent. Maya, or this dream of worldly life, is instructive. That which is subject to time, space, and causation, to change and relativity, to pain and pleasure, to sorrow and misery, is maya. It has value but not permanence. As a dream helps you work through emotions and desires, the worldly dream, maya, creates opportunities for you to grow and work through habits and desires. You wake from it, and it disappears. You wake into realizing Atman, and this plane of existence disappears into a misty memory.

Atman is the real Self, but one's knowledge of

the real Self is separated by the different, relative aspects of the mere self. These relative aspects of mind are both the barriers and gates to the higher Self. According to eastern philosophy, the mind has four main faculties. The first is *ahamkara*, or ego, the part of yourself that defines you as 'I,' with 'me' and 'mine.' The second is *buddhi*, the higher mind, the aspect of discrimination that knows, decides, and judges. The buddhi is like a mirror that catches reflections of all the sense organs and perceptions, and all thoughts and cognitions of the mind. Buddhi discriminates and compares one thing with another. The third is *manas*, or the lower mind, that produces and processes data. *Chitta*, the fourth faculty, is a reservoir or data bank of impressions and memories.

There are two aspects within us all, the real Self and the mere self. The latter is but a reflection of the former. One is imperishable and beyond change, and the other is the enjoyer and the sufferer.

Yama told Nachiketa:

"The one (the Absolute) is like the self-effulgent sun, the other (the ego, or limited self) is like its image or reflection, bearing relations as between light and shade. The one is like a witness, while the other eats the fruits of its own thoughts and deeds."

The witness is Atman. The great ninth century Indian saint and philosopher, Shankara stated:

"The nature of the Atman is pure consciousness. The Atman reveals this entire universe of mind and matter. It cannot be defined. In and through the various states of consciousness — waking, dreaming, and sleeping — it maintains our unbroken awareness of identity. It manifests itself as the witness of the intelligence."

The Kathopanishad says the Atman is never born and never dies, that it is smaller than the smallest atom and greater than the vastest spaces. It is concealed within the heart of all beings. Shankara said the Atman does not dissolve when the body dissolves, just as the air within a jar does not cease to exist when the jar is broken.

Unchanging, unchangeable, birthless, deathless, and eternal, the Atman sits in the deepest chambers of ourselves and knows all the activities of the mind and of the individual. "It is the witness of all the actions of the body, the sense organs and the vital energy," Shankara said. "It seems to be identified with all these, just as fire appears identified with an iron ball. But it neither acts nor is subject to the slightest change."

The Bhagavad Gita states about the Atman, the Self:

"He is never born nor does He die; nor having been, does He ever again cease to be. Unborn, eternal, perennial, this ancient One is not killed when the body is killed. He who knows this is imperishable, eternal, unborn, unalterable...

"As a man taking off worn-out garments later puts on new ones, similarly the owner of the body, abandoning the worn-out body, dons another new one...

"Weapons do not cleave Him, fire does not burn Him, the waters do not wet Him, nor does the wind dry Him.

"He is uncleavable, unburnable, cannot be made wet, nor can He be made dry, the eternal, all permeating, absolute, and unmoving, He is omnipresent, omnipotent, and omniscient. He is the ancient One."

Chapter Four

Digging for Treasure

The goal of life is not the drama being played, but the lesson that it offers.

Out of the tumult of human life comes the decision to look for lasting peace and joy. Where is one to look for this treasure, and how can it be found? Going back to the story of the angel who was given the job of hiding life's meaning, this treasure is hidden within. It also might be said that the treasure is buried under layers of ego, desires, emotions, habits, and other imbedded thought patterns. Atman, the individual's real identity, is waiting there. It takes nothing more than realization of this fact to truly know it—just be awake to it, as the Buddha taught. It is as simple as flicking on a light.

Peeling off the layers of ego, emotions, and imbedded thought patterns is not so easy. Shankara said that a treasure doesn't come out when you call it. It must be hunted for and dug up. All that is heaped over the buried treasure must be removed. The decision to look for the treasure is only the beginning of the hunt. The promise that it sits waiting within is taken on faith, but there is also a feeling, a voice calling out from what is at once a great distance and no distance at all. The debris that covers the treasure is identified as maya and the effects of maya. On ac-

count of maya, one is not conscious of the real Self. A
seeker must start the search in earnest and begin digging.

What separates a human being from his or her
true identity? What are the rocks, dirt, and rubble
under which the treasure is buried, and how does a
person go about removing them? What are the necessary tools to accomplish the same?

This digging is the reason for worldly human
existence. Knowing which tools to use and when is
the art of life. This work is life, and it is a magnificent
adventure with Atman, the treasure, as its goal.

We learn as we gradually dig, scrape, and peel
off the layers of what is not our real and permanent
nature, until finally the work is done and we know
who our true Self is. This is why we come to this world,
why we create it, why we compose the dramas that
are enacted across the globe.

The goal of life is not the drama being played,
but the lesson that it offers. Every human being is the
playwright of her or his own drama. Most people forget this. They think the dramas of their lives are created by God, or by others, or by the chance of math-
ematical probability in an inconceivably vast universe.
They also fail to remember that the drama of life is
just that, a play that is momentarily being acted out
for a desired result. Instead of understanding life as a
play, they take life to be the ultimate. Then the les-
sons promised by the drama are missed and a great
deal of pain and sorrow is experienced.

So it is. This is how our individual development
is shaped. We create and recreate dramas that we fail
to see as such dramas. We mistake them to be the
ultimate, and get tossed about in the turmoil of pain
and pleasure. Finally the day dawns that we turn to-

ward another perspective. We are able to step back and watch the drama from a distance. The pain diminishes and the wisdom and humor of the drama become more apparent.

Each person creates a stage, a laboratory, a drama — however you prefer to understand it — to penetrate the layers of barriers covering the Atman. The day will eventually arrive when we will realize our true identity as both the one who is watching the drama, and that which is being watched. There is only One, as the Upanishads state. Each individual is a wave in the single vast ocean of pure consciousness.

What are these barriers or veils between the real and the unreal, the permanent and the transitory, the transcendent and the immanent? What is the makeup of worldly life that binds human beings to its lures and miseries? As already suggested, the drama of worldly existence is the trap, but it is also the gateway to liberation. Put another way, according to Vedantic philosophy, the human mind is the obstacle to liberation, but it is also the tool that drills, penetrates, and drives one to the innermost treasure, the kingdom of Atman.

The Indian view of the mind is different from the prevailing western or European view. The West defines a human being by the mind, as with Rene Descartes' famous aphorism, "I think, therefore I am." Materialistic thinkers declare that the soul exists because of the body and as a production of the body. Indian philosophy is the reverse, "I am, therefore I think." It is not the body that produces consciousness of existence. On the contrary, it is the consciousness of existence that keeps the body alive and activates it. That which moves the mind and body is the real Self.

The body and sense organs have come out of

energy, they live by it, and ultimately go back into it. This energy is subject to evolution and is the source of our intellect. It has produced the intellect, the mind, and the sensory powers, which are but the different modes and forms of expression of energy. Vedanta maintains that first there is pure consciousness, and mind is a spark from or a reflection of that consciousness. Consciousness and energy produce the ego, and the Absolute is the source and background of the entire Self and the entire universe.

In other words, in the West the mind is sovereign, while in the East, consciousness is. According to Vedanta, the mind serves, or must be trained to serve, consciousness. In the West, mind is preeminent. These viewpoints define the difference between the cultures of Europe and North America, and that of India.

The external orientation of the mind in the West has led to the prosperous industrial age of the last two centuries, and the development of highly advanced technologies and scientific achievements. Material prosperity and consumption of resources are the established hallmarks of western civilization. The results of western culture are impressive, as far as they go, but the West's philosophical approach is limited. Because the West relies on the outward turned mind, cultural knowledge and experiences are limited to the realm of sense perceptions. This philosophy is too restricted to explain the mystery of the Self. It neglects to take into consideration the inner world, where pure consciousness resides in its eternal glory. The dilemma is apparent. An outward turned culture can build towering skyscrapers, transplant hearts, and walk in space, but are its people any closer to true peace within themselves or within their communities? Has this culture done anything to reduce the fear of death? By fostering all the means to deny and run from death, even to the end when it hides its elderly in nursing and retirement homes, does this culture cause the fear of death to be magnified?

The inner world is the focus of Vedanta and the Upanishads, and the goal of life is peace, happiness, and bliss. Indian philosophy describes the mind as a group of four functions called the internal instrument, the *antahkarana*. These four functions or faculties were mentioned in the last chapter, but their processes must be explained further. There is the ahamkara, or ego; the buddhi, which is the intellect or higher mind, which discriminates, knows, decides, and judges; manas, which is the lower mind that produces and processes data, the importer and exporter through sense perceptions; and finally, the chitta, the subconscious storehouse of impressions, emotions, and memories. These four faculties are meant to work together in harmony, with each faculty doing its particular job. With training and discipline these four are coordinated, and they comprise a very useful tool in the search for Atman. Poorly coordinated, differentiated, and untrained, they comprise a formidable obstacle on the path

So the first thing is to know the different aspects of one's mere self, to train those aspects, and to know they are not the real Self. Kathopanishad explains this by the metaphor of a chariot; the spiritual Self is the owner of the chariot, and the body itself is the chariot. Buddhi serves as the charioteer, using the mind as the reins to control the senses that are, as the horses, running unrestrained in the open fields of the sense experiences. Most often, unfortunately, we fail to comprehend this metaphor and are not taught how the mind functions. We do not know what to train or discipline.

The nature of manas is limited to asking whether

this or that data should be imported or not, or should be exported or not. Manas should only ask, "is this good for me or not?" Manas should be communicating these questions with the buddhi, and the buddhi should be trained and sharpened to have the answers and to communicate them to manas.

Without training, manas assumes too much power, ignores the buddhi, and acts independently, when it is not reliably capable of doing so. Manas is full of conflict within and without. Without the help of purified buddhi, manas is a source of uncertainty and misery. Over time the actions of manas become habits. This is one reason Indians repeat the famous Gayatri mantra. A portion of the mantra asks the Almighty to enlighten the intellect, which is to say to improve the functioning of the buddhi: *Dhiyo yo nah prachodayat.*

Another problem with an untrained mind is the inappropriate authority undertaken by ahamkara, the ego. The nature of ego in an untrained mind is to believe that it is the owner of the mind and the center of being. So powerful is the untrained ego that a person forgets that his real nature is divine, ultimate, and eternal. When manas tries to do a job it is not capable of doing well, buddhi is not consulted, and the ego believes itself to be the ultimate, human misery is the result.

Understanding these functions of mind is what St. Paul was referring to when he wrote: "Be not conformed to this world, but be transformed by the renewing of your mind, that you may know what is that good and acceptable and perfect will of God."

Paul did not say to destroy or repress the ego. He used the words transform and renew. Manas has a role to play, but a limited one. Buddhi has a job to do, so employ it. The ego is useful, but its role is limited, not everlasting. The ego is like a lattice framework to operate from in the world. It is not concrete, as we wrongly think. It is simply an aspect of mind, with a function. Ego is not one's identity. It is the sense of "I" called the ego that divides us into separate and individual entities. The ego gathers together all our sensations and molds our individual identity. Although it is the creator of our identity, the ego is not the ultimate reality. The sense of "I" or the ego is the blending of two factors — one changeable, the other unchangeable. The changeable factor is the foundation of the phenomenal universe, of the body and its sense of external objects, and so on. It is the source of evolution.

Manas and ego are like precarious weeds in the mind. They take over if they are not attended to. Manas says to do this, do that, lie about this and you will stay out of trouble, steal this and you will get ahead, enjoy this pleasure and you'll be happy. The ego says, yes, this is great, this is for me, and I am all that matters.

This path of doing whatever manas wants and ego says it needs, will end in pain, fear, and more ignorance. This is the path of having, needing, getting, keeping, of me, mine, and I. Ego says this body is mine, this house is mine, this spouse, these children are mine. This sense of mine and thine separates the individual from other individuals, dividing the world into them and me. It also separates the individual internally, putting up barriers to the true Self. It creates a fear of death. Death will mean the end to these things we own and want. That is scary. The prospect of the body dying is terrifying if we think we are the body, because then death seems like the complete cessation of our existence.

However, when buddhi is trained and used, a

person questions: Is this thing really needed? Is this object really required? What is the body? Buddhi teaches that the body is no more a person's identity than the reflection of sun on the surface of a calm lake is the real sun. When the discriminative aspect of mind called buddhi is trained, a person becomes aware that transitory life leads ultimately to suffering. The buddhi begins to explore and then concludes that a life aimed towards what is not transitory will lead ultimately to a life of nonsuffering.

Once the buddhi is trained, the choices that seemed murky to a person earlier become evident. Before buddhi and the art of discipline and discrimination are well employed, reason leans toward what is pleasurable. Buddhi sheds light on temporary pleasures and on the futility of gambling one's life on that which will not last. Buddhi then begins to direct the person to the course of action or thought necessary to carry one to the higher Self. Buddhi will ask what is the relationship of the ego with the higher Self. And so on.

When the buddhi is not allowed to function, the Self remains hidden. Life is wasted in a futile effort to satisfy manas and ego, which are merely aspects of the inner instrument, the total mind. Manas and ego are tools for the human being, but when they are allowed to take over they become master.

The fourth faculty of mind is chitta, the vast unconscious sea in which are stored our impressions, thoughts, desires, and feelings. What bubbles out of this sea is what we've put into it lifetime after lifetime. For most people chitta is like a great soup with a huge variety of ingredients, some dominating others in their flavors or textures, some negative, some positive.

These ingredients in the chitta affect our behavior, thoughts, and actions. We may have strong desires, for instance, for ice cream, or react strongly to certain personalities, prefer certain climates to others, or have emotional responses to particular stimuli. These desires and reactions seem out of our control, as if coming from out of the blue. These thoughts and feelings are not out of the blue at all. They are coming from within and are accessible and can be controlled by us. First we need to know, or at least be willing to accept as a reasonable thesis, that there is within our minds this tremendous storehouse of feeling and experience. As fact or thesis, we can act upon it, test it, and probe it.

Access to the subconscious mind comes from calming the surface, the conscious mind. There is nearly always some degree of turbulence on the surface of the mind, the mind bounding from one thought to another, from this to that, then back to this. Sometimes the turbulence is great, and other times the surface is calmer. There is nearly always activity in the conscious mind that prevents access to the subconscious mind.

Knowing how the mind functions and training it properly is the real duty of a human being. This is spiritual work because the properly trained mind is what allows the divine within to reveal itself. It is this duty and obligation that brings peace and joy to a human being.

The first step is to remember what our real identity is. We are not our bodies, emotions, thoughts, egos, or mind. We are Atman—divine, pure consciousness. Our bodies, minds, and egos are meant to serve Atman. If we don't know that truth, isn't it at least worth accepting as a theory that we are divine and eternal? Isn't the possibility of divine nature worth an exploration? Isn't it a critical question in knowing the relationship of life and death? What dies? What lives? What cannot die?

When it is understood that Atman is the essential nature of a person, one can begin the work of clearing the way to Atman. Access begins with understanding the framework of the mind and the makeup of a human being.

The second step is understanding the four aspects of mind and its functions—buddhi, ahamkara, manas, and chitta. In the untrained mind, manas assumes roles that are inappropriate for it, and ahamkara, the ego, takes a greater position of power and authority than is its rightful place. The ahamkara is really a temporary structure that gives form to the individual. The ahamkara is not lasting. It is not the true identity of the individual, but a servant with a tendency to think it is master.

The four faculties of the mind must be integrated. Each has a necessary role to play, in concert and harmony with the others. Manas and ahamkara should do their jobs and no more. Buddhi must be trained and exercised to make the decisions that bring a person to growth and joy.

To accomplish this integration of the faculties of the mind a further understanding of mind and emotions is required. Four basic urges determine personal emotions and their effects on the mind. Primitive, fundamental, and shared by all human beings and other living creatures, these urges are for food, sleep, sex, and self-preservation. From the standpoint of these urges, there is not much difference between human beings and other animals. The difference is the preeminence of the human mind in its ability to control these urges.

Other animals are subject to these urges. Their

lives are determined and led by them. Human beings, on the other hand, can control these urges by proper use of manas and buddhi. If the faculties of mind are not working in harmony, these four basic urges will express themselves in dysfunctional, unbalanced, and generally unhealthy ways. Eating disorders, addictions, and sexual excesses affect a person's physical and emotional health. Too much or too little sleep, or fitful sleep have similar effects on emotions and health. The fear of death, which is the central issue of self-preservation, leads to a wide variety of fears, including fear of loss of belongings, possessiveness in relationships, or fear of flying and other phobias. These disorders and addictions, with all of their emotional complications, also get fed into the chitta, shaping personalities and creating habits for years and even lifetimes.

When all the faculties of mind are truly integrated a person can soar to the higher levels of enlightenment. No great person has ever attained Self-realization or enlightenment without total integration of mind. This integration requires effort, practice, and skill. It means making the mind one-pointed and inward. Unless the mind is integrated it cannot perform skillful actions, because the finer cords of the thinking process and desires will remain obstacles in the path of liberation.

Begin the process with some sense that within you is Atman. You will come to feel the Atman and realize it is your best friend. Conduct a dialogue with yourself. Remind yourself of your real identity. Converse with yourself. You will discover that the best of all friends in the external world or anywhere else, is your own Self. If you learn to have an internal dialogue you will become comfortable with yourself. Fears of the outside world, of others, and of circumstances, will disappear. Then the presence of Atman will gradually make itself more apparent.

This dialogue requires introspection. With any close friend you are interested in their life and you are sensitive to their emotions. You listen to them. The same should be true in your relationship with yourself. Pay attention and inspect your own feelings and thoughts. Be gentle with yourself, as you would be with any good friend. Don't condemn yourself or be judgmental. You will begin to trust your inner Self and realize what a magnificent guide and constant, faithful companion your inner Self is.

Finally, it is necessary to calm the mind. As said earlier, when the manas is untrained and the ego is left unrestrained, the mind becomes turbulent and uncontrollable. At the same time the contents of chitta keep bubbling up and surfacing into consciousness. The individual becomes a slave to this chaos, and is jerked around on the chains of erratic emotions and powerful desires.

This turbulence has to be calmed. Calmness can be established with meditation. When a person's body is still and the breath is quiet and even, the mind can begin to concentrate. When the concentration is held, the conscious mind becomes more and more calm, and clarity of mind grows deeper and deeper.

When this kind of meditation is achieved the real work begins of cleaning out the mind, emptying it of old desires, thoughts, and fears, and completely integrating buddhi, ahamkara, manas, and chitta. With complete integration, the mind realizes that pure consciousness is everywhere and is sovereign. Then the mind surrenders as it realizes that all its power and authority come from pure consciousness, the source of life. Ego vanishes and death is defeated.

Chapter Five

Learning to Die

Death is not the end of life, but simply a pause in a continuing story.

Yama taught Nachiketa that it is necessary to understand death to understand life, and likewise life must be understood in order to understand death. Nachiketa learned that death is not the end of life, but simply a pause in a continuing story. Death is merely a station stop like Grand Central Station in New York City—just a place to get off a particular train and prepare for another.

This is not to diminish the meaning of life or death. How life is led, in other words the train we choose on the way to Grand Central, determines what state of mind we will be in when we arrive and how prepared we will be for the next transition in our journey. We could pick a disorderly, poorly run train, or a neat clean one. We could pick one with all sorts of attractions and distractions, dancing girls and video games, and opportunities for wealth and fame. It would be difficult to leave that train once we were hooked on all the distractions and sensual gratifications. We could alternatively pick a train in which we learned to enjoy the natural sights along the way, so that when it comes time to leave the train at Grand Central, we could do so effortlessly and joyfully.

31

Nachiketa is an example of someone who picked the right train. He would have no other train than the train of knowledge. Nothing else interested him. Long life, wealth, the opposite gender, and children paled against his desire for the knowledge of Reality and the secrets of life and death. To Nachiketa only those secrets were worth having.

The eternal nature of the Atman who dwells within is the central theme of the Upanishads. This is the secret of the mystery of death, and the key to understanding life: God pervades all, and God is the Atman animating our soul, the life of our life. Atman is everlasting, unchangeable, and therefore not subject to death. Only that which is perishable is subject to death, the perishable is there only to serve as a tool in the discovery of what is imperishable.

It is the body that dies, the garment that provides the covering for the soul on its visit to the worldly plane. The inner Self remains unaffected. It does not and cannot die because it is eternal.

As the Bhagavad Gita states: "He is unmanifest, is not the subject of thought, and is said to be incorruptible; therefore, knowing Him, it does not behoove you to grieve after anyone."

It is sad to lose what we care about in life. When someone we love dies, it is sad. Grief for that loss is appropriate but that grief should not be prolonged. Excessive mourning is unhealthy. Grief should not consume a person, because loss and death are inevitable. That is why in some cultures and religious systems a time limit is put on grief. For instance, observant Jews follow stages of mourning. After the burial of a loved one, close family members remain in mourning seven days. During this time they do not leave the house except for emergencies and do not shave or cut their hair, or put on new clothes. They are not allowed even to sit on chairs or wear shoes. Their grief is allowed to be concentrated and their mourning focused. A less intense twenty-three-day mourning period follows. For some Jews an eleven-month moderate mourning is observed.

We grieve the deaths of those close to us, and fear our own passing. There is a period for mourning, and a time to let go. This is why cultures around the globe and throughout history have devised customs of letting go, of mourning, and of putting death into perspective. These customs help people to go on with their lives and prepare for their own deaths. Human life is a cycle of coming and going, birth and death. The death of the body is not the end of the soul. The Self is unchangeable. Therefore, grief beyond the limits of its own time is unwise.

If what matters to a person is that which is passing, death looms large and horrible. Death means the end to what was central and meaningful to that person. The pain in that philosophy is profound. If, however, a person learns to let go of what is passing, whether that means letting go of objects or relationships, and seeks only that which is eternal, death is not frightening. It is just a turning, a change of clothing. So grieve, but not for too long. The same advice applies to anything that is lost—a marriage, a job, friends, a home, a dream. Grieve for it, and then move on.

The fear of death and the pain associated with death are intrinsically linked with attachment to the passing world of names and forms. As ironic as it is tragic, people seek objects and relationships in the world in a way to deny death, to comfort the reality that their worldly lives are temporary. The treatment is worse than the ailment. It is just these attachments to objects and relationships and the belief in the need for them that strengthens the fear of death. The changes inherent in objects and relationship make their loss certain. Instead of comforting their owners, these changing, decaying, and dying objects remind people of the death they fear—death of their attachments to their bodies, thoughts, habits, objects, and relationships. These attachments create, recreate and reinforce the fears of recurrent loss and death. They make life miserable and death frightening. The key to freedom from misery and fright lies with undoing the attachments.

All of life's events try to teach that out of death comes life. In the process there is an urge to know and feel something that cannot die. Jesus taught that "whosoever will save his life shall lose it, but whosoever shall lose his life for my sake shall save it." In the next sentence Jesus asked, "For what shall it profit a man, if he shall gain the whole world, and lose his own soul?"

Jesus meant that whoever is attached to the wordly life and this earthly body will lose them in death. But whoever lets go of attachments to this worldly life and this earthly body and identifies with the permanence or God-consciousness that Jesus represented, will never die. What good will it do to have all the riches of the world and all the world's pleasures? They will all disappear in the flash we call a human lifetime. Focusing on the pleasures of the world keeps the mind too distracted to search for the inner Self.

Buddha's four noble truths state that life is suffering, the suffering has a cause, there is a cessation of suffering, and there is a means to that cessation: a solution. Buddha' s solution was to live life correctly and to travel through life productively and enjoyably.

This path requires dealing with the desires and attachments that are the cause of suffering.

"For him who is wholly free from attachment there is no grief, much less fear. From craving springs grief, from craving springs fear; for him who is wholly free from craving there is no grief, much less fear," said the Buddha.

Another Buddhist text states: "Through the abandonment of desire the Deathless is realized."

"Put to death what is earthly in you," said St. Paul.

Commonly we get the message early in life that happiness is earned by acquiring things and getting something from relationships. Things are lost, relationships change, and pain is the consequence. We have a parade of emotions and thoughts that we identify with, and this brings pain. We think we are our bodies, and when our bodies are sick or they age, or we watch the bodies of others get sick or die, we experience pain.

Pain is an alarm system that indicates that something is not in balance. What is the pain of lost objects, changed relationships, shifting emotions and thoughts, and deteriorating bodies telling us? One possibility is that is simply how life is. We arrive here, strive to obtain whatever we think we need, and suffer pain in the process. End of story. That doesn't make much sense though. If someone felt pain in his foot, and the pain alerted him to an infection, would the person simply say, "Well, that's the way it goes — have a foot, get an infection." The infection would spread through the leg and kill the person. That's not rational. The person would use the pain to identify an issue in his body that needed attention. He would see it as a problem that needed a solution. Life's pain is telling us that we are perceiving our relationship to things, people, feelings, thoughts, and bodies incorrectly.

We are dependent on those things, people, feelings, and bodies. We identify with them and are attached to them. When they go or change, we feel pain. These attachments, along with ignorance, are the source of the fear of death. The more we are attached, the greater is the fear we have of death. Those without any attachments — those who do not perceive themselves as owning anything in their lives and who know that their bodies are just instruments — they are free from fear.

What does it mean to be attached to or to identify with something? Attachment means we believe we need something for our existence. This is the ego operating. It says, "I am so important and I need to have this car. This car is mine, this car means I am successful, this car helps identify me." Or, "I need a relationship with this woman. Without her I cannot be happy. If she leaves me I will be forever broken, and life will be meaningless." People get attached even to the idea of things. For example, in American culture people have been raised with certain images of what life ought to be. They see themselves from the time of childhood growing up to have wonderful marriages, living in white houses with picket fences and flowers, and having devoted children. They see themselves getting bigger houses, second cars, second homes in resort areas, and retiring early. These are the ideas the culture creates, and when these things don't come about to match their ideas, they are miserable. They feel as if some bad trick has been played on them.

This is identifying with images. You see yourself, your identity, as this person in the white house with flowers and a perfect life. You think that is you.

But that is not you. Don't be attached to these images. Learn to flow with life and all of its ups and downs.

The same tendency works in the lower mind with emotions. We get angry, and we think, "I am angry." Who is angry? To say "I am angry" is to identify with the emotion, to believe that the emotion is us. We cannot be an emotion. As humans we are capable of having anger and experiencing anger, but we are not anger or any other emotion.

Similarly, we are not our bodies. We have bodies. They are instruments for our use. We say, "I am 6'1" and blond with blue eyes." We are not that. Yet this is what we think. When someone criticizes our appearance we feel hurt. When we see our bodies getting older and slowing down, it scares us. Most of us remain in body consciousness and that is why we identify ourselves with the body. When one learns to separate the mortal self from the immortal Self, the faculty of discrimination dawns.

Death does not touch the real Self. That is difficult to believe only because we so strongly identify ourselves with our bodies and the world around us. Just because we are not conscious of something does not mean it doesn't exist.

Yama says to Nachiketa, "When all desires and passions are removed, when perfect stillness prevails, the mortal becomes immortal." That is the key. Death cannot mean an end because death has no effect on the Self. The cycle of life and death is not a random, unfortunate reality. It is an instructor. The Taoist philosopher Chuang Tzu stated:

"Birth is not a beginning, death is not an end. There is existence without limitation, there is continuity without a starting point. There is birth, there is death, there is issuing forth, there is entering in. That through which one passes in and out without seeing it, that is the portal of God."

Life is an ongoing Upanishad that directs a person to search for the eternal and identify with what is permanent, not with that which is impermanent, and thereby overcome death.

According to Vedanta we exist not because of our bodies but because of our very being. The inner self creates the body. During sleep we are not conscious of our bodies, but still we exist. Materialistic thinkers turn it the other way around. They look to the body, declare it is evidence of our being, and assume if there is an inner being, it comes by way of the body. Vedanta says just the reverse. Consciousness makes our body appear to exist.

Death is not something to fear but its function in life should be understood. Accepting death is a reality that will help you to realize that this life here is temporary, that the world is only a platform, that you have come here on a journey to learn and grow, and then the journey ends.

St. Paul referred to life as a slight, momentary affliction that prepares a person for eternal glory. "Everything in human life," he said, "is for spiritual work." In somewhat darker imagery, but with a similar message, Chuang Tzu said to "look upon life as a swelling or tumor and upon death as the draining of a sore or the bursting of a boil."

At the same time remember that God, or the eternal Reality, is within you. Death reminds you not to attach yourself to this world. Learn from the world and let it go. See your body as just an instrument. It serves a purpose and then its work is done.

Chapter Six

Living on Purpose

We are all making a sacred journey to our true, divine natures.

Fear is removed and life is enjoyed only when there is a purpose in life. We need to ask ourselves if life has a purpose. What is the meaning of life? Usually we begin asking this question when we have experienced a great deal of pain after suffering the loss of property or relationships. We've seen the emptiness in getting more material wealth or fame or power. We've seen how fleeting the pleasures of those are. We've begun to say, "If wealth, fame, and power do not give happiness, then what does?"

Out of our pain we begin to suspect there is something more to life, that life is not limited to what our senses experience. We may only suspect. Our knowledge of anything beyond the world of forms — that which we see and hear, and so on still may be barely a whisper deep within us, but the possibility is worth the exploration.

The exploration begins by establishing the philosophy that there may be something more to life. That philosophy at least gives a direction. With a philosophy life takes on more meaning and immediately begins to take a different shape. The intention to learn more provides focus and focus gathers energy. There is joy in that alone.

With only the vaguest of goals and our motivation still only a whisper, we begin to see the objects and relationships in our lives differently. They are no longer the center of our lives The pain inherent in the loss of them, or in the fear of loss of them, is not so intense.

Having such a philosophy that suggests a greater meaning than owning and keeping changes life's atmosphere. A sense of freedom grows. Gradually we begin to detect that it is not owning and keeping the things of the world that matters, but something else — perhaps giving and letting go.

Yet these thoughts remain only faint sounds within us, especially since we have heard all our lives so loudly and distinctly that acquiring possessions and wealth and power, and having sensory pleasures, are topmost in priority for a good life. Nonetheless the faint inner sounds continue.

The second step is to reorganize one's life. As with all great transitions of mind and changes of old habits, the second step is done gradually, as personal capacity allows and grows. For instance, as the shift is made from a philosophy of acquiring objects to one of a greater purpose, our needs diminish. Materially, life becomes simpler and less burdensome. Following a philosophy that life may have greater meaning, we begin to see that we don't need relationships with others in the same ways. We don't need others to give us something. We don't depend on relationships for what we can get from them. We can be more free in our relationships and the emphasis changes from needing and taking in a relationship — whether marital, parental, filial, or any other — to giving. Emotionally, life becomes lighter.

This philosophy and reorganization usually mean our lifestyles become less opulent and require fewer distractions. More is given away. Less is needed. Concerns for health change. Ironically it seems to be those who are most afraid of dying who do the most to hasten the process by eating rich, heavy foods, ingesting too much alcohol, and smoking. Their fear of death draws them to the sensory pleasures that bring death about more quickly. With a philosophy that says there is more to life, we naturally shift to a healthier diet and more exercise.

Other changes also come about. As we expand from the narrow viewpoint that the priorities in life are material and sensory wealth, to a greater view of life with spiritual purpose, then not only do we change in lifestyle habits and relationships, but we see the world differently. If we no longer think we were dropped somehow by accident onto this planet to get all we can, then we see that is also true of all other people. If we are here for a greater purpose, then so are all five billion plus inhabitants of the planet. Our sense of community changes. Our family grows. We realize we are part of a global community, all brothers and sisters on a long journey, though on different paths.

No longer can we do work that might harm other people, or harm the world in which we all live. If we have jobs that pollute the environment, or create difficulties for other people, we will feel obliged to find other work.

At the same time we no longer feel threatened by the differences in other people. If all five billion people on the planet are here for a higher spiritual purpose, then the differences in race, color, and beliefs are ultimately superficial. These differences, along with everything else happening on the planet, are serving the higher spiritual purpose. Race, color, and creed are part of the different paths toward the same goal. The fear that these varieties of race, color, and creed once held, that somehow people who were different were a threat to what is owned, disappear. In eastern philosophy this wide angle reorganization of a person's life is called *dharma*. One sense of the word dharma means to organize one's life in such a way that individual action is in harmony with interpersonal relationships and with the community, local and global. It implies morality, righteousness, and virtue. A life that is led with unselfishness, harmlessness, compassion, non-possessiveness, and non-covetousness in personal relationships and toward the greater global community and earth itself, is a spiritually healthy life. However, if a person is selfish, harms others, brings harm in some way to the community, and feels a sense of possession of things and people, such a person's life is contracted, and spiritual progress is hindered.

Another interpretation of dharma is the notion of destiny. Dharma is a person's duty in life. Put another way, dharma is the path a person takes to best use this life to most effectively reach the goal of life.

A person's dharma is related also to personal *karmas* and *samskaras*. What does a person need to earn, burn, and discard in order to move forward in spiritual life? What is the dharma that can effect that learning and burning? Whether that dharma is to be a carpenter, social worker, fireman, nurse, computer technician, mother or father, Californian or Italian, it doesn't matter. From a general point of view, no dharma is better than another. From the standpoint of making spiritual progress, being a small vegetable farmer or street cleaner is as valid and efficient a dharma as being president or pope. Each person has a dharma that best suits his or her spiritual needs.

It is vital then to look for and establish a personal dharma that provides a personal set of values to follow and develop, and identifies those duties that will be helpful in the process of personal growth.

In this exploration of something beyond worldly life it is necessary to find a spiritual path. We all need a guidebook into the geography of the heart. We are all making a sacred journey to our true, divine natures. Although that divine nature is so close and so known to us, it also remains hidden in the tangled recesses of our thoughts and desires.

All the religions and spiritual systems of the world come from the human aspiration to know the truth about our real identity. Within each of these systems are maps to that Truth that is shared by all. Some maps are written in Sanskrit, others in Latin, Hebrew, Arabic, or Chinese. Some maps take sea routes, others overland or air. Some guide followers this way up the mountainside, others that way. They all, however, come to the same pinnacle of Truth.

We usually find ourselves in those systems that represent our culture. Religions evolve out of cultures to serve the spiritual needs of people in the context of their lifestyles, environments, and histories. Islam emerged from a particular culture, history and community need. The same is true of Buddhism, Christianity, Judaism, and all the religious systems of the world. None is better than another. They merely reflect cultures, times, and needs. Hinduism in reality is a way of life and a philosophy of life. It is not a religion.

As the world has shrunk with sophisticated communications systems, it has become easier to share the knowledge of religious systems with other cultures. There has been a mixing of ideas and techniques that

44 / SACRED JOURNEY

are benefiting people throughout the world. The great movement of eastern philosophies in the second half of this century throughout the United States and Europe is an example of this sharing.

However, it is important to remember that spiritual disciplines that have become religious systems have been reinterpreted. Institutions have emerged that have become something other than the spiritual imperative that gave rise to the institutions. Jesus said he was not creating a new religion; he was simply telling the truth. A religious system developed and concealed the truth told by Jesus. The truth is still there, but around it is this new institution and its interpretations of truth.

Jesus said, for instance, "I am the way, the truth, and the life; no one comes to the Father but by me." He meant that the way to eternal life, or Brahman, is by knowing the Atman, the pure Self that is embodied by all. The institution that formed seized on the statement and used it as an institutional bludgeon, demanding that people join that institution and take on its dogma or be doomed.

So is the case with Islam. Internal research of Islam has been done by the Sufis. The Sufis have dived deep into the Islamic scriptures and emerged with gems of wisdom. I find that all religions have one and the same truth to share with their community. The fortunate few who have realized this truth know that it is priestly wisdom and churchianity that have created confusion.

The same phenomenon has happened in all spiritual systems. The institutions are meant to protect the truth, and they grow to bind a community together. That's the meaning of religion from the Latin *ligare*, to hold or bind together a culture or people of like beliefs. However, often the institution takes on a life of its own, ignoring the truth it meant to teach. The institution and its leaders become more vital than the truth itself. This leads usually to politics, prejudice, dogmatism, factionalism, and sometimes bloodshed with one religious group fighting another. The mentality develops that, "We have the truth, you don't. God is with us, not you." All manner of injustices and harm in the name of religion come from this attitude. The egos of religious leaders create a situation where their followers worship them, or fear them, and the purpose of the path is forgotten.

The desirable path is that which responds to the true spiritual needs of the individual, not to the demands of an institution, and not to the whims of institutional leaders. In truly spiritual systems both the institutions and their leaders exist solely to serve the spiritual needs of their members and followers.

Chapter Seven

Chains or Freedom

There is nothing in your life that is not your choice, your doing, your karma.

After establishing an individual philosophy, re-organizing your life, and finding your dharma and spiritual path, there are two other preliminary steps on the spiritual journey.

You are to take responsibility for your own life. This point seems especially important in America these days, where so many people are in the habit of blaming someone else or something else for their unfortunate situations. Their parents may have abused them, neglected them, or in some way failed to appreciate or understand them. They say the result is their own unhappy marriage, difficult relationships with their children, or career failures.

Perhaps the parents were abusive, neglectful, or misunderstanding. They did their best with what they knew. Undoubtedly there is a link from one generation to another. If a parent is abusive with a child, there is an effect. However, when a child realizes the cause and effect, then it is time to begin releasing the parent from blame and responsibility. Until that happens the child cannot progress. Until then, he or she is bound to the past.

The same kind of blaming goes on toward siblings, spouses, and children. It goes on toward the government, the educational system, culture, and history. Whatever is wrong in a person's life is blamed on unfair sibling relationships, uncaring spouses, needy children, taxes, imperfect schools, or having been born at the wrong time.

Understand your relationships, your government, and your history, but let go of blaming. There is nothing in your life that is not your choice, your doing, your karma. That may sound harsh but it is a liberating reality. If everything is your own doing, and your choice, and everything is right for spiritual growth, then nothing is really wrong. Everyone has an opportunity to grow. There is nothing to fear.

The word karma has come into the mainstream usage in western culture. Regrettably, however, the word is often not used accurately in the West and its meaning is frequently twisted. In modern western society's new lexicon, the word karma has come to be used very casually and incorrectly to mean fatalism, something utterly out of one's hands. People say, "Oh, it's karma, there's nothing you can do," or, "it's not your fault, it's bad karma."

Implied in this interpretation of the word karma is the belief that whatever happens is not a person's doing. It's all due to fateful karma. This view takes the responsibility for an individual's life and circumstances and places it on an abstraction called karma, as if it were some ill wind blowing through that forced its effects on you.

This is not what karma means. Karma is not a catchy word from the East that lets you off the hook. Karma places responsibility for your circumstances and experiences with you. Karma means that you are responsible, you determine your circumstances. You are the architect of your present situation, and past, and future. It is not meant to create guilt. To accept responsibility for your life gives you the power to move, change, and grow. It means you are independent. Your life is not dependent on what others do or think. You are not a victim of circumstances, parents, selfish spouses, inconsiderate children, tyrannical bosses, economic depression, or world politics.

In the philosophy of Vedanta the phrase 'victim of circumstances' is not possible. These circumstances we find ourselves in are of our own design and intent. According to Vedanta these circumstances, whether we label them good or bad, pleasant or unpleasant, are the opportunities we have created for our growth. In the purest sense, that is all there is — just a steady parade of opportunities from which to learn and grow. It starts with understanding karma and knowing that we are completely responsible for our lives.

Another way to see this is to understand life as we do our dreams. It is accepted that our dreams are our own creations. They come from our subconscious minds, out of our thoughts, desires, and fears. These dreams can be useful to us. They are natural ways to help us work out emotions and unfulfilled desires. The waking state is no different. The circumstances of waking life are created by us to provide the opportunity to grow toward realization of our divine nature. The keys to growth lie in those relationships and situations that give us the most discomfort. These relationships and situations repeat themselves, not out of bad luck, or 'bad karma,' but because uncomfortable situations and relationships represent the barriers to our freedom. Freedom comes when we overcome these self-created barriers.

It bears repeating that these barriers are neither

useful nor harmful. Western culture refers to these barriers as sin and people as flawed. It is important to state here that the western hemisphere suffers because of the notion of sin. Yoga science and Vedanta refer to these barriers as obstacles. In these philosophical systems there are no commandments, only commitments that are to be understood in the proper perspective. The concept of sin does not inspire self-confidence or sense of purpose. It reinforces the idea of the eternally imperfect human being and encourages a fatalistic approach to human existence. From this viewpoint, if there is any freedom to be had, it is in the hands of the Creator, not the individual.

This is not the Vedantic view of human life. Think of a flower that grows from a bulb. Certain conditions make it possible, indeed necessary, for that flower to bloom into its full splendor. Among the conditions that are needed are a bulb, dirt, moisture, and certain temperatures to be maintained for a period of time. Some might say the bulb is a crusty, shriveled, unattractive thing that lives in a grimy, soggy, bacteria-filled environment. When it blooms into its unique beauty, God made it so. Some western religious attitudes describe human life as unclean, and any beauty comes from an outside God. Vedanta says that it is just nature. The bulb is simply what it is, and certain conditions are required for it to come to full expression of its splendid and perfect nature. Likewise, a human being is simply on a natural course toward expression of the perfect Self. Each person is in just the right conditions for that growth toward perfection to occur.

Karma is a way to express these conditions. No one is free from actions or karma. To do, say, or think anything is karma. The word also means that what is sown is unavoidably reaped. The two definitions are linked. Every action brings a reaction. Every cause has an effect. Every thought, word, and deed carry a specific outcome. Whatever actions we have performed in the past produce their fruits in the present and future, and that is the real cause of our pains and sorrows. Once the arrow is shot it must go to its destination. As long as the arrow is in our hands, we can choose its course. All the wrong deeds that we have committed in ignorance in the past produce their adverse effects. We should be careful not to commit the same mistakes again.

This philosophy is not meant to make people tremble at the prospect of the consequences for every mistake they have ever committed. Consider again the concept of karma from the standpoint of describing something very natural and very logical, as the steps in the process of evolution.

Vedanta takes a long view of the process, and this view explains the mystery of death—the mystery Nachiketa wanted explained. Nachiketa knew if he could understand the mystery of death, the meaning of life would become clear.

The mystery, according to Vedanta, is that there is a single intelligent consciousness that comprises everything that is, was, or will ever be. All the names and forms we identify and call pieces of the universe are fragments and shadows, reflections and glimmers of pure consciousness.

The purpose of human life on this platform we call worldly existence is to discover fully, that Reality. Worldly existence is just an apparent construction for the individual to make his or her way to Reality. Karma is like a rope that keeps us tied to the construction we created called life.

We can say that karma is the source of misery. We can focus on karma as suffering from the consequences of actions. We can say karma is what shackles us to this world and all its painful imperfections. There is another perspective, a higher view. We can see karma as the curriculum we must take to achieve the clarity of pure consciousness. Nothing more. Follow the rope of karma through the maze we call life and find the absolute Reality. Until Reality is found, we keep moving through the maze, or back to this platform of worldly life. At the risk of working these metaphors too much, we take a set of courses in one lifetime, and return in another life for more courses, again and again until we finish the self-imposed assignments we refer to as karma. Death is simply the end of a semester, or the comma in a long sentence. Karma might be viewed as a burden, but another way is to see karma as a natural guide, instructive, and inevitable.

Yama told Nachiketa that those who dwell in the darkness of ignorance and are deluded by wealth and possessions are caught in the snares of death. These beings will travel back and forth from death to death. Karma is the boat that carries a person back and forth. It is a necessary vehicle until the journey is finished. The law of karma is inescapable, and it does not end with worldly life. When a person dies he carries the seeds of the law of karma with him. Death doesn't change it. Death only means that the outer aspects of human life, the garments of flesh, bone, and blood are discarded. The finer substance of the human being — thoughts and feelings, and karma — continue.

All the thoughts and feelings and the karma of a person are stored within the subtle mind. The impressions that find their way from actions and thoughts into the bed of chitta are called samskaras. The actions the samskaras in turn provoke, the personality characteristics they shape, and the habits and likes with which each person finds himself or herself, are called *vasunas*.

We are speaking now of the wheel of karma, the ongoing movement of the individual from lifetime to lifetime. We act, we think, or we desire and a groove is etched in the mind as a particular sort of memory. The groove is a samskara. The more we act a certain way, think, or desire, the deeper is the groove etched. The tendency that springs from the memory is the vasana. The deeper the groove, the greater the tendency. A person with a strong tendency for anger has deep anger grooves, for example. More anger means deepening the groove, strengthening the hold of that tendency and karma.

Karma is not God's doing. Karma is performed by each individual. It is what each particular individual must deal with, understand, and complete. Karma is the product of each person's own actions, thoughts, and desires. No one else is responsible for it. It is absolutely precise. There are no accidents. Everything is finely, utterly balanced. In the short view, life does not seem at all perfect or just. Why do some people seem to suffer more than others? Why, for instance, are some people sick and others healthy, some people are wealthy and others are poor? Seen from the vantage of the precision of karma, life is perfectly just. Life is exquisitely perfect the way it drives people in their evolution.

If a person's life is seen as an organic spaceship making its way through eons of time and infinite spaces toward a thumb-sized target billions upon billions of light years away, the slightest miscalculation in navigation will send the craft far off-course. Karma is the built-in device for navigational correction. It brings a person back on course. No matter how far off-course a person may stray, karma will make all the necessary adjustments, though they may be harsh, and guide the person on the most narrow course toward the tiny target.

Karma can be divided into three parts: the karma performed in the past, the karma being performed in the present, and the karma that will be performed in the future. Indians say if you want to know a person's past karma or past actions, look at his present life. If you want to know a person's future, look at his present actions. Nothing can be done now about the karmas performed in the past. Those are arrows already shot, some have already landed, some not yet. Accept the consequences of those past karmas and learn from them.

It is a mistake to think that there is no free will, that the entire universe and what happens to anyone and everyone are predetermined by something called karma. There is free will. That is the point of karma. Those arrows that have not yet been shot are still in the quiver of our will. We choose which arrows to shoot and when. We decide and act. How we do so determines the future. Something or someone apart from us does not decide our fate. The future is our own design in all its detail, good or bad, sorrowful or joyful. We chose how to live in the past by what we did, said, thought, and desired. We are choosing now in the present. Karma is the law of cause and effect, but free will enables us to eventually transcend the bondage of the law.

This is reassuring and empowering. Instead of placing blame for life's circumstances on God, fate, or others, a person takes full responsibility. The power of growth is in that. From life to life, and circumstance to circumstance, a person creates and chooses what is needed for growth at any given moment in the long evolution toward enlightenment. Each soul chooses the parents and family situation he or she needs, the role in society, and the mix of ease and discomfort, to provide the perfect opportunity for progress on the path toward freedom.

This process of karma folds and entwines again, and the future is shaped by how the individual handles the present. It may take lifetimes for certain karmas to unfold and get burned. The outcome depends not on God, on others, or on luck, but on one's own response to one's karma. As a person learns to accept with equanimity his or her circumstances, whether pleasant or unpleasant, they can look forward to the future with joy and courage. They rise above their karma. If pains and sorrows are the result of past actions, to avoid suffering in a future existence, the wise person will stop committing any more deeds that lead to suffering.

The law of karma is uncompromising and all are bound by it. However, there is a way to cut the rope of karma and to overcome death. The way is to live skillfully and purposefully. Finding the way to purposeful, skillful living comes gradually, as we understand the source of the pain and sorrow we spend our lives trying to overcome. Gradually we come to understand the nature of death, which we inherently fear. Unfortunately people often direct their lives from this fear.

When people act out of fear, they create karmas and samskaras that are born of fear. These samskaras encourage more fear, unless they are dealt with. If a person identifies with the body, they will fear sickness, the aging process, accidents, walking across the street, meeting strange people, or any other manner of possible harm. Consequently, everyday life will inevitably attract the harm they fear. These fears will become habits, which will gravitate the person toward danger and sickness. If a person believes their identity is their job, any changes to that job will be a threat to them. If they lose their job, they lose their identity. If a person's identity is as a parent, that identity is challenged when the children grow up and leave home.

People's actions are based on these fears. Their lives are molded around them. Their fearful actions and thoughts reinforce the fear itself and sow new and stronger seeds of fear for the future. A powerful, imprisoning cycle spins. Only a person's choices can change that cycle. The bonds of karma must be broken. That is the responsibility of the individual. It requires strength and courage.

The secret of life and death involves not only seeking to know what is our real identity. Unraveling this mystery also involves our actions, words, and thoughts, and how and why we perform these actions, utter certain words, and think particular thoughts. Performed one way our actions can bind us to earthly life and an endless cycle of births and deaths. Done another way, actions can create joy in life and victory over death.

Remember that you have chosen this life. You have moved toward this moment of discovery in your journey. This is the perfect time for you to live in the world to make the most spiritual progress. The people in your life, your parents, children, spouse, friends, colleagues, are perfect for your growth.

Our whole lives in the external and internal worlds are motivated by our samskaras, the impressions left by our thoughts, actions, and choices. No one punishes us for our good or bad deeds, but our samskaras motivate our present actions. We sow what we reap. When we understand this motivating force in our lives, we cannot blame others, nature, or God for the lives we lead. Our lives are our own creation. Our problems are our own. We shouldn't fight with ourselves over these problems, but try to understand them. We should understand our relationships with others. It is not helpful to blame others for what is not right in our lives. What have we brought to the relationship? Why have we chosen it? These questions lead to an expansive view of the situation, to compassion, and to selflessness.

Without a larger spiritual context, this world is not perfect. That is its nature. It is a world of change, death, and decay. Anything in this world cannot hold ultimate happiness because it goes away, breaks down, and changes. You cannot rely on this world, its objects, or relationships for happiness because they are not reliable. They cannot be reliable because they cannot last and remain the same forever. That is not the nature of this reality.

This world is a training ground, a school, a play. It is perfection in its imperfection. As a place to learn and grow, the worldly plane is incomparable. It is your consummate creation, shaped from your individual deeds, fitted to your individual needs.

Chapter Eight

Paths of Freedom

People seek the fruits of their actions because they don't know their real needs, and they don't have faith that all their real needs will be met.

In the previous chapters some preliminary steps in the journey to immortality have been described. First there has to be an idea that there is something more than what we have limited our identities to, and an individual philosophy must be established. It doesn't have to be elaborate, just an inclination toward something beyond life is a start. The person reorganizes his or her life to move with that inclination. At the same time the inclination itself pulls the person toward changes in lifestyle, behavior, and thought. Then the seeker begins to focus on his or her dharma or duty in life. Relationships are approached differently, with emphasis on the aspect of giving and less need for getting. Finally, personal responsibility is taken for one's life. This is the groundwork of a spiritual life, a life that is lived fully, richly, and with purpose, toward that transition called death.

Besides these preliminaries to a spiritual life, there are two other fundamental prerequisites: *vairagya* or nonattachment, and *abhyasa* or practice (of techniques) for spiritual growth. The two are linked, each complementing the other. Abhyasa is the subject of the next chapter.

Vairagya is translated variously as nonattachment, detachment, or dispassion. It should not be confused with indifference, lack of emotion, lifelessness, numbness, or anything of that sort. Vairagya is hardly indifference or numbness. Vairagya is a vibrant, open, expansive way of living. It could more accurately be defined as love, as a wonderful energy of openness, freedom, joy, giving, selflessness, and fearlessness. That is vairagya.

The Vedantic philosophy of vairagya says you own nothing, so there is nothing to fear. Everything you need for the purpose of life is there in abundance. There is no reason to be possessive and selfish. There is no reason to worry. Just live life as fully as possible with what you have. Jesus said it clearly: "Take no thought for your life, what you shall eat, or what you shall drink, nor for your body, what you shall put on. Is not life more than meat, and the body more than raiment?

"Behold the fowls of the air, for they sow not, neither do they reap, nor gather into barns, yet your heavenly Father feeds them. Are you not much better than they? Which of you by taking thought can add one cubit unto his stature?

"And why take you thought for raiment? Consider the lilies of the field, how they grow; they toil not, neither do they spin. And yet I say unto you, that even Solomon in all his glory was not arrayed like one of these. Therefore, if God so clothed the grass of the field, which today is, and tomorrow is cast into the oven, shall he not much more clothe you, oh you of little faith?

"Therefore, take no thought saying, what shall we eat? Or, what shall we drink? Or, wherewithal shall we be clothed? Your heavenly Father knows that you have need of all these things.

"But first seek the kingdom of God, and his righteousness, and all these things shall be added unto you."

Don't fret over the things of the world. They are not there to be acquired and hoarded. They were meant to serve spiritual needs. If spiritual progress is the focus of life, everything you need, whether it is a lot or a little, will be there. Vairagya is the expression of this faith.

Technically the word vairagya means control over desires. As Buddha explained, desires are the cause of suffering in the world. Buddha meant desires in a broader sense of attachment as well. Desires hook and attach people to things and to others, making them dependent and defining the meaning of life. Suffering is the only result. Therefore, to rise above suffering, according to Buddha, rise above desires. To rise above desires sounds impossible, or not even healthy or human, but it is possible to control and transcend desires.

In the Vedantic philosophy there is only One, pure consciousness, Atman, Brahman, or however the It is defined. If that is true, then desires are irrelevant, because there is nothing to desire that isn't already there. The one who desires is also what is desired.

The reality of human existence is that as long as we don't fully identify ourselves with Atman, we will have desires. The route to Atman is through overcoming these desires. That requires vairagya, which has two paths, the path of renunciation or the path of fulfillment and selfless action. There is also a third, or middle path, which is to balance renunciation and fulfillment.

Renunciation is harsh and very difficult. It is the

rare person who can look at all worldly pleasures, all things transient, and say, "These things and relationships, the pleasures of the senses, cannot bring me to God so I will have none of them." It is a treacherous path like the razor's edge. This is the path of monasticism, and a person must be fully prepared for it. Preparation means a person has tasted pleasures for lifetimes and has realized that they ultimately leave a sense of emptiness and lack of fulfillment.

Renunciation is a path of fire. The renunciate is purified of worldly attachments. The ordinary person who is filled with desires cannot jump into renunciation and declare he will give it all up. The fire will consume him, not the desires. Not only desires are involved, but also the fuels and byproducts of desires—all the disappointments of life, greed, lust, hatred, passions, anger, jealousy, and so on. All of them need to be renounced, and they cannot be renounced without having the strength of spiritual discipline.

Renunciation is for the person who has already burned many worldly desires. Much spiritual practice has already been done. The seeker is prepared and is strong enough to bear the heat of the fire of this path. A person cannot just pick up one day, leave his duties and family, and declare it is time for the path of renunciation. If he leaves with all his imagination intact, all his deepest thoughts firing, and his mind undisciplined, he has not truly renounced.

This rather so-called renunciate will walk down a road and see ghosts and demons in the dark because he did not deal with his fears first. He does not have the knowledge and wisdom to walk the path of renunciation. Running away from home does not make anyone a sage. Failing to meet responsibilities does not make anyone enlightened. Simply escaping from the world will not bring you to God.

Renunciation is a path of self-sacrifice and self-knowledge. When a person comes to this path, he has realized the limited value of worldly objects. He knows these objects are valuable only as long as they serve the purpose of achieving the higher goals of life. He knows the mind runs after the tantalizing objects of the world only as long as it does not know that the true treasure lies within. He has experienced some insight and has enjoyed the calm and tranquillity that comes by becoming aware of the inner treasure. From the perspective of a calm mind he not only sees the dangers of the attractions of the world, but realizes in meditation the more deeply buried, latent attractions and desires, and knows their dangers and disorienting natures. He knows that the fire of renunciation is appropriate.

This path requires much self-training and self-discipline. Many latent desires lie hidden in the mind. This is why the path is referred to as walking the razor's edge. With every step there is a chance of falling. Selfish desire is the strongest of all the obstacles encountered by the renunciate, or anyone, for that matter. Only those who have gone very far toward fearlessness and freedom from the charms, temptations, and attractions of the world can tread this path. It is so demanding a path that it requires a high degree of fearlessness and freedom and the ability to make the mind one-pointed toward enlightenment. Nothing short of these great demands will lead to success.

It also bears mentioning how sweet and enjoyable the path of renunciation is. When one is prepared for it, when much of the energy of outward turned desires is turned inward, the resulting joy is incomparable and indescribable.

The other path of vairagya that is equally essen

tial for spiritual growth is the path of selfless action. On this path one performs one's duties, one's dharma, skillfully but selflessly. She knows she has actions to do, as everyone does. She does them with full attention but not for any personal gain or glory, or for any sort of return. She is not concerned with that. She does the duties and that is all. In this way the seeker on the path of action learns to live in the world, but remain above it.

The goal of both paths, of renunciation and action, remains the same. Both aim for enlightenment. Both paths seek to fully mine the treasure of vairagya. The strong golden thread of nonattachment and control over desires runs through the path of renunciation and the path of selfless action. On both paths the seeker is trying to follow that powerful thread through the maze of life to enlightenment.

People seek the fruits of their actions because they don't know their real needs, and they don't have faith that all their real needs will be met. Most people scurry around in their lives doing this or that action, expecting to be paid and praised. Both are traps that bring an individual deeper into confusion. There is no freedom in this kind of life. It's like climbing onto the wheel of a rat's cage, spinning faster and faster, and achieving nothing but exhaustion.

The goal of life is spiritual. Understand that as the guiding principle of your life. With an attitude of cheerfulness and with full attention, do your duties in life in your role as student, worker, child, parent, member of the community, and so on. Then let go and leave the rest up to the timeless process of spiritual unfoldment. It won't seem like work or duty, and everything will be in harmony.

This approach simplifies life and expands it; it purifies the seeker from karmas and attachments.

There is no longer any concern for collecting odds and ends from your actions, piling up belongings, or needing reinforcement from others for what you've done. Your needs become less. Your sense of owning and having grows less and less. At the same time you become increasingly selfless. You do your actions greased with love. Great joy comes when actions are done with love. Personal gain is not the motivation behind your actions. Slowly you learn to do your actions selflessly. To do this is a spiritual discipline, a spiritual practice.

Chapter Nine

Practice, Practice, Practice

Approach your life whole-heartedly.

The twin side of vairagya is abhyasa. Abhyasa means practice and practice means discipline and attention. The two are linked as night and day. A person cannot develop nonattachment or vairagya without abhyasa. Similarly, abhyasa without vairagya amounts ultimately to a waste of time.

These two, nonattachment and practice, are the most powerful vehicles for spiritual progress. Separately, they are like a boat with one oar. There is movement, but little progress.

In the preceding chapters the preliminaries to a spiritual life were discussed. These steps constitute the broad strokes on the canvas of your spiritual life. They are the essential background. The more refined strokes, from which the sharpened images and details come, are created by abhyasa or *sadhana*. Sadhana is spiritual practice, and usually refers to the specific practices of a tradition—*hatha yoga, pranayama* or breathing exercises, repetition of *mantra,* and so on. Abhyasa is a more encompassing term that includes not only practice of specific techniques, but the overall goal of life and the application of belief systems. In this book the two terms are used almost interchangeably.

To begin understanding abhyasa remember you are the citizen of two worlds — the outer world of family, community, and dharma, and the inner world you wish more fully to explore. Abhyasa begins with balancing these two worlds. Living in the external world, learning and growing, yet remaining above so the whispers from the inner world can be heard, is the sadhana of a person's life. When a balance is achieved between the inner and outer worlds, the outer world can be used to gain access to the inner, and the inner world facilitates a richer and fuller life in the outer world.

Jesus was completely balanced. He was in the world but above it. He was both human and divine, as all human beings are. His great importance as a public spiritual figure was to show humanity that they are divine because they are human, and human because they are divine. Jesus demonstrated his divinity out of full expression of his humanity.

As the Kathopanishad suggests, humans are not so much bodies with souls as they are souls with bodies. The divine is immanent in humans and humans are inherently divine.

Living a spiritual life does not require escaping from the world. It is not useful to look at the flaws of the world and say it is ugly and sinful. Turning away from the world will not lead to spiritual happiness. Live in the world. By living fully in the world with all of its apparent imperfections one can attain spiritual perfection.

Along with the effort toward balance and non-attachment, practice selflessness. Selflessness is an art that requires much practice to perfect. Strength, non-attachment, love, and fearlessness grow from the practice of selflessness.

Make it a part of your daily life to do things for

others without anyone knowing. To be selfless and attentive toward others is not so much an effort as it is a very natural way of being. At the same time, do not forget yourself. In the observances of yoga the first principle is *ahimsa,* non-harming. This principle is not meant to be applied only to others. Ahimsa should first be applied toward yourself. You should not harm yourself or allow yourself to be harmed by others. Be sensible in your non-attachment and love. While it is not helpful to be ego- or me-centered, it is also not beneficial to be exclusively you-centered. The Upanishads teach that all is One.

Approach your life wholeheartedly. Whatever you do, do with your whole heart and fullest attention. When you are with your children, be with your children, not your work. When you are at work, be with your work, not your children. Be in the moment at hand, not in the moment or day that has passed, or in the moment or day yet to come.

Be decisive. Exercise your buddhi, that aspect of your mind that chooses, makes judgments, and decides. It is a very powerful part of mind. Make the best decision you can, and take action accordingly, leaving the outcome up to the divine force. Choose your friends, activities, and livelihood wisely. All of them should be compatible with your higher goals.

Be gentle with yourself. This is a long and difficult journey. Your goals should be reasonable so as not to create frustration and disappointments. Be willing to crawl before you walk. Perfect each skill as you move along on the journey, and forgive yourself when you stumble, or even slide backward. Setbacks are temporary and meant to be instructive. Let yourself slide backward, observe what has occurred, get back on your feet, and move forward. Sliding backward is part of the pattern of growth. Just don't slide back and stay there. Don't ever give up. Progress is made with perseverance. Never lose hope.

Pay attention to your body. This is part of sadhana too. Eat well. Eat whole, natural foods. Sleep well with a regular schedule. Exercise regularly. Your body is an expression of your mind. What goes into your body and how your body is treated affect the functioning of your mind.

Your breath requires attention, too. The breath carries the vital energy called *prana*, the life force. Prana is the energy that animates you as a human being. Without it you cannot live for a second. Your health and vitality are determined by how well and how balanced the prana flows through you. An imbalanced flow of prana affects the body and the mind. Prana is like a suspension bridge between the body and mind. If prana, carried by the breath, is harmonious and even, the bridge is still. If the prana does not flow evenly, the bridge sways and swings, making the journey from one shore to the other uneasy, upsetting both body and mind.

Control the four basic urges of food, sex, sleep, and self-preservation. Understand how these urges operate and learn to channel them. From these four primitive fountains spring the six mainstreams of emotions: desire, anger, pride, attachment, greed, and egotism. The manner in which these basic urges are understood and integrated determines the flow of basic emotions.

Another fundamental practice is the cultivation of contentment. Many westerners grow up believing their lives ought to be perfect. That will not happen. That is not the nature of life. Life is always changing, shifting, decaying, dying. That is its nature. To accept and understand that is the way to contentment.

Life's so-called setbacks, as well as its so-called

victories, are the same from a spiritual point of view. When the disappointments of life come along, treat them as instructive. There is a dark side to life, and everyone casts a shadow. The shadow shows the way to light. Don't hide from the shadow, but don't try to cling to it either. Examine and accept your dark side. Treat your setbacks, misfortunes, as well as victories and what you call good fortune, with the same equanimity.

Contentment is a wonderful way to stay focused and preserve energy. Discontent breeds unhappiness and negative emotions that expend energy and disturb concentration. This is not to say you should be satisfied. Contentment and satisfaction are not the same. You should not be satisfied until the goal is reached. The journey should be made with contentment.

In abhyasa follow three golden rules:

1) Be aware of the goal and work toward it all the time.
2) Make the best use of your time.
3) Be happy in every situation in life.

The goal of these practices is to calm and focus the mind, and elevate the mind beyond worldly attachments. This is a process of purification of the mind, to clean it of all the habits that keep the mind running outward toward various desires.

To truly do this work of calming, focusing, and purifying, the student needs the practice of meditation. This is the practice of concentrating the mind and learning to even out all the mind's fluctuations, all its dips, turns, and eruptions. Concentrating the mind gives the individual a tool to focus on the mind itself, to penetrate this formidable power to reach the real Self.

An aspirant must first intellectually distinguish the transitory aspects of his personality from the Atman. A person's true identity is not the mind or senses, but the Atman. Atman is hidden beneath layers of habits, desires, and fears. So entrenched are these habits and thoughts, that the layers have to be penetrated by the disciplines of concentration and meditation, before Atman can be realized. Meditation is a means of collecting all the scattered forces of the mind and bringing them together in one powerful laser-like force that can cut through the mind to reach the Atman.

The Atman is not recognizable through the senses, and cannot be discovered through learning or sacred teaching. Subtle, deep, and eternal, the Atman is revealed only through the disciplines of concentration and meditation that purify the mind.

Meditation leads the seeker past the layers of the senses and the limited mind, where habits, desires, and fears live, to the superconscious state of samadhi where the seeker comes face to face with that which is immortal. When Atman is realized, the seeker rises above pain and pleasure, and sorrow and misery, the conditions of the transitory world. Where Atman is, death has no access. Atman is the realm of the Absolute, the realm of the infinite, and it is only as far away as our inner depths.

Meditation is not sitting and fidgeting, daydreaming, worrying or fantasizing. It means watching, calmly observing the mind itself. Calm observation makes the mind itself calmer. The calmness of the mind creates the power to go deeper and deeper into the beds of samskaras, into all the latent memories and impressions that daily provoke our habits and personalities. However, by calmly and very quietly going to the samskaras and observing them they are burnt away; they bubble to the surface and dissipate. This is the process of purification. It is a very powerful practice, and an essential one. Meditation is the exact method of becoming aware of who you are. It is the fundamental training for knowing your inner world.

Throughout all of these practices, another practice or tool is employed. It is *sankalpa,* the Sanskrit term for determination. It means: "I will be decisive. I will be wholehearted. My growth is certain. I know I will make mistakes, but I will pick up and continue." This is the attitude of sankalpa. So important is the practice of sankalpa that no real progress can be made without it. If you doubt you will move ahead, you will prove the power of doubt. You will not progress. Sankalpa, however, will swiftly dispatch you to your goal. The scriptures state that with the help of sankalpa nothing is impossible. Say what all great leaders say, "I will do it; I have to do it; I have the means to do it." Decide that no matter what happens you will do what you set out to do. If you are determined, potential distractions will still be there but you will continue on your path and remain undisturbed. You cannot necessarily change your circumstances or your world, family, society, or friends to suit you, but if you have strength and determination, you can go through this procession of life very successfully.

As the process moves forward the mind is treated as a laboratory. The individual begins to watch the movement of emotions and the procession of thoughts and gains increasing control over them. The aspect of witness, the presence of Atman, begins to make its presence known.

Also with practice comes greater power of intuition or buddhi, the higher mind. This power is essential on the spiritual path. With a mind calm and focused through meditation, charged with and armed with contentment, the powers of the mind expand. Intuition helps to guide the spiritual seeker on the journey and show him that he is not alone.

The process of purification, according to the Kathopanishad, takes place through discrimination, knowing the choices and making the right ones; through discipline so the proper choices can be absorbed and assimilated to make the aspirant stronger and more determined, and through meditation.

Finally, there is grace, that comes after all the above effort. Discrimination, discipline, and meditation are preparation for grace. Just as a host prepares his house for a special guest, the Kathopanishad says the Atman, the special guest, will come when the house is prepared.

The preparation is difficult, but the difficulty makes the treasure more glorious, and the seeker more worthy of its attainment.

Chapter Ten

Divine Grace

Grace dawns when action ends.

In the effort to understand life and approach death meaningfully, vairagya and abhyasa are the responsibility of the seeker. When these two are truly undertaken, another help follows. That help comes in the form of *guru* and grace, each linked to the other, each so beautiful and comforting, each so powerful. Unfortunately, each is so frequently misunderstood.

Western culture, which has increasingly welcomed and embraced traditions from the East in the last thirty years, has too often understood guru to mean simply a teacher. In the West guru is frequently considered to be merely someone who is trained in philosophy, meditation, and hatha yoga. From this point of view, the guru is expected to share this knowledge with the students, training them in scriptures and various spiritual disciplines. While the western student may become dependent on the teacher and have high expectations about what the teacher should do on behalf of the student, the guru is nonetheless viewed as a teacher only.

In ancient times students received formal education in *gurukulas*. The students lived with their guru from an early age and were given not only instruction on an intellectual level, but also were guided in spiritual development and in the maintenance of physical health. The guru had a very close relationship with the students and knew their habits and level of inner strength.

In today's life there is no spiritual environment in which a seeker can fully concentrate on learning the language of silence in order to find inner fulfillment. It is very difficult for the student not to be distracted by the temptations of the external world. Modern education focuses on memorizing facts of the external world, and ignores the growth and development of the inner being. The gurukula system of ancient times is not practical in today's world, but a more holistic approach to education can be adopted. Such an approach emphasizes spiritual growth along with the development of the intellectual aspects of the mind, and also includes guidance in how to maintain the fitness and health of the physical body. In the eastern tradition guru is much more than a teacher. He or she represents the special energy that is guiding individuals toward their fulfillment as human beings, toward perfection. Grace is the impulse of that energy.

The word guru is a compound of two words, *gu* and *ru*. Gu means darkness and ru means light. That which dispels the darkness of ignorance is called guru. The energy and action of removing darkness are guru. Guru is not a person, it is a force driven by grace.

To put this another way, there is an intelligent momentum that pervades the universe that is moving all human beings toward the perfection we call God. Guru is that intelligence. Everyone's receptivity to that intelligence varies. It depends on preparation, which includes the development of vairagya or non-attachment, and abhyasa or practice. In other words, guru is always there, but the student may not be ready to receive what the guru has to offer. When the student is prepared, the guru always arrives to help the student do what is necessary to progress in removing the veil of ignorance. It is said that when the wick and oil are properly prepared, the master lights the lamp.

Guru is not a person, but guru can be represented in a person. One who has developed his or her own spiritual awareness to a very high level can guide others, and is considered to be guru. Only one who is finely attuned to the inner guide can inspire the awakening of the inner guide in another. Guru is not a physical being. If a guru begins thinking this power is her or his own, then they are no longer a guide. The guru is a tradition, a stream of knowledge.

In India guru is a sacred word that is used with reverence and is always associated with the highest wisdom. The guru is unique in a person's life. The relationship between disciple and guru is like no other relationship. It is said that guru is not mother, father, son, or daughter. The guru is not a friend in any conventional sense. It also is sometimes said that the guru is father, mother, son, daughter, and friend all in one, the guru is sun and moon, sky and earth to the disciple.

The truth is that the relationship of guru to disciple is indescribable. The relationship extends to the realm beyond the world, transcends death, and stretches far beyond the limited karmic bonds associated with family and friends. A mother and father help sustain the body of their child, and nurture and guide the child through the formative years of life to adulthood. Guru sustains, nurtures, and guides a soul through lifetimes to ultimate liberation.

The relationship with the guru is based on the purest form of unconditional love. There is complete openness with the guru. The disciple should hold nothing back from the guru. This is why in the tradition, a student goes to the guru and offers a bundle of sticks to burn. The bundle symbolizes that everything the disciple has is offered unconditionally to the guru. Everything is offered to the guru so the guru can do the work of shaping the student spiritually. The disciple comes with full faith and entrusts his whole life to the guru. The guru takes that life and chops it and burns what is not necessary, and then carefully carves what remains into something sacred.

In this chopping and burning, the guru is merciless. The guru's job is not to hold hands with the disciple and wipe away tears, but to cut into pieces the disciple's ego and all that stands between the disciple and freedom. The guru does not allow dependence. If the disciple becomes too dependent on the guru, the guru pushes the disciple away, insisting on independence. It is a remarkable expression of the deepest love.

To be on a spiritual path with a guru is not an easy thing. It is not pleasant. The guru tests the disciples, puts them in the most difficult situations, and creates obstacles for them. All the tests, difficulties, and obstacles are meant to train and expand the consciousness of the disciple.

That is the sole work of the guru. The guru wants nothing from the disciple. Guru is that force moving a soul toward enlightenment. The guru's actions are from pure compassion. As the sun shines and lives far above, the guru gives spiritual love and remains unattached.

Guru is a channel for spiritual knowledge. Jesus repeatedly reminded his disciples of this. "I have not spoken of myself, but the Father who sent me." The Father is that stream of pure knowledge. Jesus, as an enlightened being, was attuned to that knowledge.

No human being can ever become a guru. Guru is not a human experience, or, better said, guru is not a sensory experience. It is a divine experience to be a guru. A human being allows herself or himself to be used as a channel for receiving and transmitting by the power of powers. Then it happens. Then guru manifests. To do that, a human being must learn to be selfless, must learn to love. Real love expects nothing. That is how genuine gurus live. Selfless love is the basis of their enlightenment, and the basis of their roles as channels of knowledge.

Guru is not the goal. Anyone who establishes himself as a guru to be worshipped, is not a guru. Christ, Buddha, and other great persons did not set up any such example. Guru is like a boat for crossing the river. It is important to have a good boat and it is very dangerous to have a boat that is leaking. The boat brings you across the river. When the river is crossed the boat is no longer necessary. You don't hang onto the boat after completing the journey, and you certainly don't worship the boat.

Many times students come to the guru with a preconceived idea of what the guru should be like. They come with expectations of what the guru is there to do for them. Perhaps the students think the guru should give them much attention, or make decisions for them, or take on troubles they have created for themselves. Sometimes the students think the guru should behave in a certain way. When these expectations and preconceived images are not met, the student becomes upset and may even leave the guru.

This is not the proper way to approach a teacher. A student should not be filled with expectations and preconceived images, but with a burning desire to learn, and with firm determination. Then there will be no difficulty. The guru and the disciple can then do their work accordingly.

The spiritual seeker should not worry about who the guru is, or what the guru will do. The seeker's first concern is getting prepared, organizing her or his life and thoughts in a spiritually healthy way, and then working toward a way of life that simplifies and purifies. At the right time the master will be there.

Once the guru has arrived, the methods and behavior of the guru should not be the disciple's concern. The disciple's work is to act on the instructions and teachings of the master, and at the same time work toward more and more selflessness and surrender of the ego. It is the ego that is the principle barrier to enlightenment.

A spiritual master's ways of teaching are many and sometimes mysterious. To one student the guru may show much attention, spending much time with a student, even doting on a particular student. Another student may be utterly ignored by the master. It doesn't matter. Each student is getting a teaching, and because of the insight of the master, just the right teaching at the right time. The guru is not in a student's life to give the student what the student thinks she wants, but rather to give what is needed to progress spiritually.

Jesus' parable of the prodigal son illustrates this. Briefly retold, a man had two sons. One day one son asked for all the property and wealth that would come in his inheritance. Then he went away and lived a wild, sensory life of rich foods, drink, gambling, and women. When all of that wealth was spent, the son returned. The father ran to his son when he saw him, and hugged and kissed him. He gave him expensive clothes to wear and ordered a feast to be held.

Meanwhile, the other son had remained all this

time with his father, working for him and beside him, always respectful and devoted. When the devoted son saw all the attention given to the wayward and reckless son, he asked his father how this could be.

"I've been here all these years with you, always serving you, obeying every commandment, and you've never so much as given me a goat to throw a party for my friends. Now my brother returns after squandering all that wealth and living a wild life, and you treat him like a king and make a grand celebration for him."

The father's response was essentially that the wayward son needed this attention at this time, and the devoted son did not. Each son was given what was right for his spiritual growth at the right time.

The guru does not operate from what seems fair, or outwardly appropriate. He is not constrained to such cultural amenities. He can seem harsh, even brutal. He will put students in situations that make no sense, or are very uncomfortable. He will say things that won't make any sense for months. He will ask things of students that students think are impossible. Everything the guru is doing is for the growth of the student. The student need only have faith in that fact.

The guru also teaches without words or actions. As the disciple learns to surrender and move the ego out of the way, and grows more selfless, the ability to learn intuitively from the guru grows. The student learns in the cave of silence. It is like tuning into the guru's frequency or plugging into that stream of knowledge. The guru is always working from there. The disciple's role is to gradually learn to also work from that place. The disciple learns this by doing all duties with love, by being non-attached, and by surrendering. The disciple should always be striving to purify and prepare for more and greater knowledge. Then

God will say, "I want to enter this living temple that you are." Remove the impurities and you will find that the one who wants to know reality is the source of reality.

There is also the activity of grace. Grace is the impulse or the impetus of the energy to dispel darkness. There is the grace of the scriptures, from the wisdom that has passed down from others. There is the grace of the teacher, who imparts that wisdom and helps bring it to life in the student. There is the grace of God, or pure consciousness, that is alive and everpresent in everyone's life. Integral to these three graces is the grace of oneself, having the will to undertake a purposeful journey in life, to do the spiritual work of life, and to prepare oneself.

How do we get this grace? It comes of its own when a seeker has made maximum effort. When all efforts have been made, and all efforts have been exhausted, then grace comes.

A Sanskrit word for grace is *shaktipata*. *Shakti* means energy, and *pata* means bestowing. Shaktipata means "bestowing the energy" or lighting the lamp. Sometimes shaktipata is translated as "descent of power." A power comes from above, of its own, to a vessel that is cleaned, purified, and is prepared to receive it. When the instructions from the guru have been completed, the seeker has become strong in selflessness and surrender, and the samskaras have been burned, grace comes.

In my own life, since I was a small child I was raised and guided by my master. I had done all that he asked of me. Grace had not come and I grew frustrated. So one day I went to my master and said, "You have not done shaktipata for me. That means either you don't have shakti or you don't intend to do it."

I told him, "For so long now I have been closing

my eyes in meditation and I end up with nothing but a headache. My time has been wasted and I find little joy in life."

He didn't say anything, so in my exasperation I continued talking.

"I worked hard and sincerely," I said to him. "You said it would take fourteen years, but this is my seventeenth year of practice. Whatever you have asked me to do I have done. But today you give me shaktipata or I will commit suicide."

Finally he said to me, "Are you sure? Are you really following all the practices I have taught you? Is this the fruit of my teaching, that you are committing suicide?"

Then he waited a moment and said, "When do you want to commit suicide?"

"Right now," I said. "I am talking to you before I commit suicide. You are no longer my master now. I have given up everything. I am of no use to the world, I am of no use to you."

I got up to go to the Ganges, which was near, and was prepared to drown myself.

My master said, "You know how to swim, so when you jump in the Ganges, naturally you will start swimming. You'd better find some way so that you will start drowning and not come up. Perhaps you should tie some weight to yourself."

"What has happened to you?" I asked him. "You used to love me so much."

I went to the Ganges and with a rope I tied some big rocks to myself. When I was ready to jump, my master came and called, "Wait. Sit here for one minute. I will give you what you want."

I did not know if he meant it, but I thought I could wait at least a minute. I sat in my meditation posture and my master came and touched me on the forehead. I remained in that position for nine hours and did not have a single worldly thought. The experience was indescribable. When I returned to normal consciousness I thought no time had passed.

"Sir," I said to my master, "please forgive me."

With that touch my life was transformed. I lost fear and selfishness. I started understanding life properly. I wondered if this experience came about because of my effort or my master's.

His answer was simply, "Grace."

"A human being," he explained, "should make all possible sincere efforts. When he has become exhausted and cries out in despair, in the highest state of devotional emotion, he will attain ecstasy. That is the grace of God. Grace is the fruit that you receive from your faithful and sincere efforts."

Grace is only possible with a disciple who has gone through a long period of discipline, austerity, and spiritual practices. When a student has done these practices and followed the teacher's instructions with all faithfulness, truthfulness, and sincerity, then the subtlest obstacle is removed by the master. The experience of enlightenment comes from the sincere effort of both master and disciple. When you have done your duties skillfully and wholeheartedly, you reap the fruits gracefully. Grace dawns when action ends. Shaktipata is the grace of God transmitted through the master.

Guru is the disciple's guide through life, through the mysterious terrain of the spiritual heart, and into and beyond the realm of death.

Chapter Eleven

Life Hereafter

Death is a solemn experience, a change from which no one can escape. One who does not prepare for it is a fool.

The discussion about life after death has been going on since the dawn of history, but no definite conclusion about the immortality of the soul can be reached by those who are on an intellectual plane and are not spiritually awakened. It is not possible to understand what exists after death by intellectual arguments or discussions. The absolute Truth cannot be scientifically proven because it cannot be observed, verified, or demonstrated by sense perceptions. The Atman is beyond sense perceptions. Scientific experimentation, confined by its own limitations, cannot reveal the highest truth. That is why the scientists cannot reach any concrete conclusions on the immortality of the soul and life hereafter, and nothing can convince them either. The materialist finds it difficult to believe that anything continues to exist after death. One who lives on sense perceptions only cannot catch a glimpse of the beyond.

One has certain expectations of life after death according to his or her religious beliefs. People dream of immortality and wish for heaven. They comfort one another with the thought that the departed loved one is now with God forever. The religious hold that in heaven there are plenty of watersheds, fruits, beautiful women, music, dancing, and so on. Followers of certain sects believe in a heaven of heroes where battles are fought against their enemies and against ferocious animals. All these heavens are nothing but mental realms where one's highest desires are allegedly fulfilled.

Everyone has certain desires that they consider to be the most delectable, and at the same time they wish for a realm where such desires could possibly be fulfilled. Therefore, the longing for a heaven projects a realm that is a replica of the heaven one has sought to achieve. This heaven is a projection of one's own ideas and desires that is no more real than are dreams. When a person dreams, she may think she is in heaven till she wakes up. On waking, the reality of the dream vanishes. Dreams and heavens are realities only under certain conditions.

The idea of heaven was conceived by the ancient seers of India, but they did not consider it to be an eternal state, as some religions do. Outside of Hinduism and Buddhism, the concept of heaven implies an eternal existence. According to Hindu philosophy, the idea of an eternal heaven is a practical impossibility. Heaven or any other kind of existence after death is not static but is determined by one's own thoughts and actions. Those who experience heavenly realms and enjoy celestial pleasures can do so only as long as their good deeds and thoughts entitle them to. There is always a limit to good deeds and thoughts, and likewise, there will be a limit to the results accruing from them. The word eternal denotes that which is beginningless and endless. According to Vedanta, heaven cannot by its nature be eternal, for all things that are subject to the laws of time, space, and causation are impermanent and perishable. All worldly pleasures are limited by time; they do not continue forever. Celestial pleasures are akin to the pleasures of the world. Even though they may be experienced for a long time, they must eventually come to an end. Those desires that cannot be fulfilled anywhere except in the world will bring the soul back to the physical plane of existence.

At the time of death the soul discards the body, its outer garment. Yama told Nachiketa that after the body is dead and destroyed, the soul continues to exist. There are spiritual realms where the soul remains without the help of the physical body or the phenomena of the material universe. These realms are not cognizable to the sense organs and can be perceived only through spiritual intuition.

Unrealized souls remain in the realm of the departed ones for an uncertain period after death. They have gone through the ordinary process of death because they could not realize the true nature of the real Self on this plane.

Much of the fear associated with death is the fear that death may be painful. The process of death itself is not painful; it merely changes conditions. Lack of preparation and attachment are the cause of the pain experienced at the time of death. Death is never painful for one who is prepared and has acquired knowledge of Atman. Such an individual remains detached from the body and bodily senses, and is unaffected by bodily changes. Death may be painful and lead to a sorrowful state when the soul is very attached to the physical plane, things of the world, or individuals. At the time of death such a soul suffers and goes through agony because it is unable to completely let go of those attachments.

Between life and death there is an intermediate state in which prana ceases functioning. If one is not prepared for this moment, he will suffer mental tortures and will not be able to explain or express anything to others. One who has known the Reality is saved from this calamity.

In the transition of death, before the external vehicle is completely dropped, those who are not enlightened experience various temporary levels or realms, pleasant or painful, respectively—depending on previously performed, positive or negative, karmas. For example, in *pitriloka* we meet our ancestors or dear ones, and in *svargaloka* we enjoy various pleasures. The Tibetan Book of the Dead and the Garuda Purana of Hinduism explain extensively the stages through which one passes in the process of discarding the body.

There are different heavenly realms, lower and higher, depending on the purity and impurity of one's mental constituents that remain even after the physical body is dropped. For the ignorant, death is a long and deep sleep, interspersed with dreamlike heavenly or hellish visions. Those who claim to communicate with departed souls are either hallucinating or lying. When someone is in deep sleep, it is not possible to communicate with anyone. Only enlightened souls can communicate with others after death because they remain fully conscious all the time.

Those who have performed good deeds, have led righteous and selfless lives, and have obtained some perfection in this life, can enjoy a clear vision of the divine Self in the highest realm. However, the wise say that the highest attainment and realization of the Self can be had only in this very life. Heavenly realms like pitriloka and svargaloka cannot reveal the highest truth. Liberation cannot be attained in these realms and the various pleasures of heaven can hinder the soul from realizing the Atman. Self-realization is possible only here in this life and not after death. Those who believe that they can realize the real Self in the realm of the departed soul after death will be sadly disillusioned. Those who do not realize the immortal nature of the Atman before the dissolution of the body lose the great opportunity which comes through a human birth. The attainment of Brahman is possible only here in this life and not in life hereafter.

According to Vedanta the human being consists of five sheaths or *koshas:* the gross, physical sheath (*annamaya sharira*), the sheath of prana (*pranamaya sharira*), the mental sheath (*manomaya sharira*), the sheath of intellect (*vijnanamaya sharira*), and the blissful sheath (*anandamaya sharira*). They are called sheaths because they cover the Atman as a sheath covers a sword. They are described as being formed of successive layers, one upon another. The physical sheath is the outermost, and the blissful sheath is the innermost. The Atman remains separate and detached from all these five sheaths.

At the time of death the physical body, along with the conscious mind, are separated from the immortal part. There are no sense perceptions after death because the sense organs are left behind with the body. Senses do not function on the subtle level.

In the process of discarding the outer vehicles or sheaths after death, one comes briefly in touch with the blissful sheath, anandamaya sharira. Those persons who have documented near death experiences are describing this brief contact when they speak of being drawn to a brilliant light that overwhelms them with love. Such experiences are possible but they have nothing to do with Self-realization or enlightenment. These momentary experiences do not have the capability to transform anyone or bestow extraordinary powers such as clairvoyance or the energy to heal others. If one remains in darkness and ignorance throughout life, how is it possible to come in touch with the Atman even for a brief moment at the time of death? If a lamp has many coverings, the light can be seen but it is very dim. When all the coverings are removed, the light is clearly visible. To see the light is not enlightenment, but to realize the light within is the real experience. This is not the light of the sun, moon, or stars; it is the light of wisdom and eternal bliss. There is no other experience comparable to enlightenment. Death has no power to enlighten anyone. The seeker should make sincere efforts to prepare for the next step and should try to attain enlightenment here and now while on the earthly plane, instead of hoping to be enlightened after death.

Ignorant souls go to heaven or return to earth for the satisfaction of their unfulfilled desires. He who desires is born. One who does not desire is not reborn. According to the theory of rebirth, a soul is born again and again, depending on the merits or demerits of its actions, so that in every successive birth it may acquire more and more knowledge, and in the end attain perfect liberation.

This theory of rebirth cannot be proved by modern scientific methods. A scientific approach can only treat it as a plausible theory which is in conformity with the laws of cause and effect, that are the very basis of the physical universe. The rishis of the Upanishads were not impressed by the theory of eternal retribution in heaven or hell, for such a hypothesis is based on a disproportionate relationship between cause and effect. Life on earth is short and full of temptations. To inflict upon the soul eternal punishment for the errors of a few years, or even of a whole lifetime, is to throw to the winds all sense of proportion. The ancient seers developed the doctrine of rebirth on a rational basis, showing that it is unfulfilled desires that bring about a soul's embodiment. The length of time the soul must spend in the transition of death before taking another body is solely dependent on the intensity of desires. There is no hard and fast rule set by nature.

Many western philosophers such as Pythagoras, Socrates, and Plato believed in the theory of rebirth. Nowhere in the Christian Bible and Zoroastrian scriptures has the doctrine of rebirth been explicitly mentioned, nor has either prophet repudiated the theory of rebirth. The reason is that during the period of Christ and Zoroaster it was a common belief.

Believing or not believing is not the important consideration for one's spiritual uplift. The fact is that if almighty God is kind and merciful and decides human destiny, there should not be any disparity in His creation. Equality is the law of the Absolute, and disparity is humanity's making. According to the doctrine of rebirth, we are all fully responsible for our lives here and hereafter. Each person is born into a world that has been fashioned through the personal karmas of his or her past.

The soul, after fulfilling its desires through the manifestation of the body, discards the body and assumes a fresh form. According to our desires and tendencies, we are born on a higher or lower plane consisting of the various gradations in the subtleties, the levels of purification, of the subtlest sheaths. We must not forget that we are the creators of our future destiny through our thoughts and deeds. It is foolish to think that God punishes the wicked and rewards the virtuous.

We do not consciously choose the factors of our next rebirth. They are determined, or chosen, by our previous actions, thoughts, and desires. This accumulation of grooves or samskaras that define a person superficially as personality, travels from one birth to the next. The grooves shift like dunes on the desert, responding to the experiences and will of the person. They change shape and influence over great expanses of time, creating different personalities and different incarnations, but all moving toward ultimate liberation. The grooves determine the characteristics of the incarnation—whether male or female, what parents, any siblings, which station in life, the lifespan with how much suffering, how much joy, and so on. There is nothing arbitrary about it. The birth is perfectly matched to the spiritual needs of the evolving individual soul.

Those who have realized the transient nature of life on earth or in heaven seek to avoid the endless repetition of births and deaths. They aspire for *Brahma loka*, the highest reality beyond the heavens from which one never returns. The realized individual remains fully aware in all conditions—while living in a human body, and during the state of death. The knower of Brahman does not go to any realm or heaven, nor does the knower become anything other than what it has always been—the Atman, the Self of all. After dropping the physical garment, the realized soul remains in a state of perpetual bliss and happiness, and infinite love and wisdom. The knower of Atman is like a person who has awakened from sleep and dreams no more; she is like a blind person whose sight has been restored. A liberated soul who has direct experience of the Atman does not come back to the physical plane unless he chooses to return to serve others. Such a *jivanmukta* is no longer tossed into the dualities like bondage versus liberation.

The enlightened soul has burned all the strands

of karma which bind other human beings. Such a one wields free will and chooses whether to be reborn or to merge with the Absolute. If the choice is for rebirth, the circumstances of that birth are also consciously selected. Such souls, according to Buddhism, are called *arhats*.

The secret that has been revealed by the King of Death is the greatest of all secrets for every human being who wishes to know where he will live after death. For ordinary mortals this remains a secret for many births to come. The mysteries of life and death and life hereafter are known to only a fortunate few.

Humanity has learned so much about the material world and how to overtake nature. They have worked hard to know the secrets of birth, and have found ways to make the process of birth easier and less painful. However they have not learned to prepare properly for dying.

Death is not frightening, but that which is frightening is fear of death. Death is like a mother that gives solace to those who have wasted their time and energy in enjoying the world—just like chewing on a husk that has very little content and does not at all quench the thirst.

Death is but a comma and not a full stop. Death is a solemn experience, a change from which no one can escape. One who does not prepare for it is a fool.

The real Self cannot die. It continues to exist even when the physical sheath is destroyed. The physical self is the gross medium that remains latent in the Atman. When the physical body is destroyed, the subtle substance of the body remains the same. Nothing is ever lost in the universe. Cosmic energy continues from eternity to eternity.

Modern science has discovered that everything in this world is but the product of vibrations which impel energy particles to attract other energy particles. Solid matter has successively been reduced to these empty particles, and then to electromagnetic waves, that have ultimately come to be understood to be forms of energy. In the philosophy of yoga, all that exists and happens in this universe is the result of motions and vibrations, the cause of which is the cosmic energy or prana. All animate and inanimate objects of this universe are made of the vibration of prana. This vibration of prana is at the root of all universal phenomena and is the prime cause of all events happening in the universe. Prana is the cosmic life principle and it has its own laws. Without prana the universe would not exist. The eminent scientist, Sir Arthur Eddington, said that we must remember that the concept of substance has disappeared from fundamental physics and has been replaced by a concept of the periodicity of waves. Modern science has indicated by experiment that the world of physics is a mental phenomenon. It is therefore no wonder that physics has virtually ended in metaphysics, thus confirming the intuitional revelations of ancient rishis: *Sarvam khalvidam Brahma* (Verily all this is Brahman).

The first manifestation of prana was space, *akasha,* which gradually evolved into the phenomenal universe. According to Vedanta there is no such thing as dead matter in the universe. The entire universe is a living organism. Yama explained to Nachiketa that whatever exists in this phenomenal world is but the manifestation of the vibration of prana. According to Rik Veda the cosmic force existed before the beginning of evolution and will continue to exist after the dissolution of the manifested universe. From one mighty source all the forces of nature have burst into manifestation. The universe is the manifestation of that One who is the substratum of the universe. There is no such thing as loss or gain of the vibration of prana in this universe.

By the power of prana and through the forces of evolution, the internal and external worlds come into existence. The whole world is eternal in its essential nature, but non-eternal in its external form. When all the external forms of the universe are destroyed, the formless substance—the mother energy of the universe—will continue to exist from eternity to eternity.

Wherever there is life, there is some manifestation of intelligence. Intelligence and life go together. This intelligence is of the inner Self, which has as its instrument the life force, prana. It is really the Self that lives and functions through the help of the pranic force.

The objective world is only one half of the universe. What we perceive with our senses is not a complete world. The other half, which includes the mind, thoughts, and emotions, cannot be explained by the sense perceptions of external objects.

The five senses are the main doors through which the individual ego comes into contact with the external world. These five senses are the gates through which we receive the vibrations from the external world. These vibrations are first carried into the brain cells. Molecular changes take place in these cells and the vibrations are in turn translated by the ego into sensations. Next, the sensations are formed into percepts, which after a series of mental processes are transformed into concepts. This goes on and on endlessly. When you think of any object, you perceive instantaneously the mental image of that thing. It is called a concept.

If an intelligent mind does not exist, there will be no perception. Vedanta describes the position thus:

"Finer than the sense organs are the sensations, but the mind is beyond, and beyond the mind is the intellect, and greater than the intellect is the cosmic ego. Beyond the cosmic ego is the unmanifested One. This is the highest path that reaches the ultimate Reality."

The pranic force has been given five names according to its different functions in the physical body—*prana, apana, vyana, udana,* and *samana*. In the human body the air which rises upward is prana, and that which moves downward is apana. Vyana sweeps like a flame through all the limbs, maintaining circulation of all fluids and energy, throughout the body. Udana conducts the soul from the body at death, and by virtue of samana nutrients are assimilated.

When the soul or *jiva* departs, it is followed by the vital energy, prana. When the prana departs, all the other life supporting organs follow. The breathing system is the vehicle of prana. It is the breath that establishes the relationship between mind and body. When inhalation and exhalation cease to function, death occurs. Physical death is a change, but it does not annihilate the subconscious mind and soul.

The subtle powers of the five organs of action (the ability to speak, to grasp, to move in the world, to procreate, and to excrete) and of the five organs of sense perception, the five pranas, the manas, and the buddhi constitute the subtle body. At the time of its rebirth, the soul is accompanied by the subtle body. The gross body dissolves at death, but the subtle body continues to exist. The subconscious mind, which is the storehouse of merits and demerits, becomes the vehicle for the jiva, or the soul. All the samskaras of our many lives remain in the storehouse of our subconscious mind in a latent state like seeds. The relation between the subtle body and the gross body is akin to that of the seed and the plant. As the seed contains all the qualities of the plant in the seed germ, so the subconscious mind retains all the samskaras of our previous lives.

The Buddhists and the yogis believe in and discriminate between the soul, the mind, and the body. The soul has not been created. It is essentially consciousness and is perfect. After the dissolution of the gross body, everything remains latent. The soul survives. Our souls remain after death. If the soul is the real entity and existence, there should be some way to experience it. Everyone who undertakes the appropriate spiritual discipline can have this experience.

Life and death are only different names for the same fact — the two sides of one coin. One who goes beyond such differentiations can conquer death and reach the other shore, that is, eternal life. A person who understands the fundamental truth that the Atman is immortal and all else is perishable, can solve the mystery of death. Life after death can be experienced here in this very life by those who have attained samadhi. Those who have realized their real Self are immortal.

Chapter Twelve

Mastery Over Death

Death is a habit of the body.

Yogic adepts have discovered that there is something more to learn from death. Death is not merely a necessary pause in a soul's journey to the eternal. It is a passageway and a tool that can be used at a person's will.

To understand this we turn again to the Kathopanishad. Yama calls the body the palace of a king. The king is Atman. Yama describes eleven gates to the palace. Seven of these gates are sensory — two eyes, two ears, two nostrils, and one mouth. Three more gates include the navel, and the generating and excretory organs. The final gate, and one that is not ordinarily known, is in the center of the brain and is called *brahmarandhra*, the fontanelle located at the crown of the head. It is the seat of the infinite, the seat of the king, Atman. From this seat, Atman guides and directs all his attendants mind, intellect, sense perceptions, and gross senses. The first ten gates are the passageways to worthy life. Brahmarandhra is the opening to divine and eternal life. In the case of the ordinary person the life force departs through any of the ten gates, especially through one that has been the seat of one's most intense desire. The accomplished yogi departs through the eleventh gate.

The Upanishads emphasize the difference and stress that the king of all these gates is Atman. Atman is that which is to be served, and the way to do that is by managing the activity at the eleven gates, by controlling the intellect, mind, and senses. Yogis know how to control these gateways and how to serve and discover Atman. They have learned to use the brahmarandhra to understand the mysteries of rebirth.

When the gateways to the external world and to eternal life are fully regulated, then the link between worldly life and eternal life is understood. The misery of death and the great pangs of fear that are associated with it disappear. When all the elements that comprise a human being, including the senses, thought waves, and the energies of the mind and body are harmonized, Atman is revealed.

Death is a habit of the body. No one can live in the same body forever because the body, like any chemical composition, is subject to change, decay, and death. To cling to that which will inevitably pass away creates fear and misery. That clinging is natural and is shared by all who remain focused on the physical aspect only. They suffer because they are unaware of the whole. Meditation, culminating finally in samadhi promises freedom from this clinging to the body. Through meditation control over the eleven gates is attained. Then a person has command over mind, body, and soul and becomes aware of the whole. The technique of meditation is free from religious dogmas.

Brahmarandhra opens only at the time of union with the Atman, and that union is possible through samadhi, the transcendental state in which no fluctuations in the mind occur, no desires, no fears, no attachments. The word samadhi means *samahitam* — no question remains unanswered, no mystery remains unsolved. Simultaneously, the chattering of mind vanishes and all languages are forgotten. In such a state the mind has no means to brood or think. This is a glorious state of mind in which the mind is absorbed in the transintellectual contemplation of infinity. Yama described the state of samadhi in which the realm of immortality is attained and the Atman is realized. He said, "When all senses are withdrawn from the organs and are silenced, when the mind is quiet and still and thoughts do not disturb the mind, in that state the glory of the Atman is realized and bliss dawns upon the horizon. That is the state of samadhi."

The highest state of samadhi is not at all similar to death. Samadhi is a state of enlightenment while death is an experience in the darkness of ignorance. In samadhi one is fully conscious, but in death there is no consciousness. For the ordinary person death is like a long and deep sleep; the soul remains attached to the mind after death, but the individual remains in deep sleep. There is no awareness. Yama told Nachiketa that samadhi "is not a state of death—it is the sameness and oneness beyond the realms of the world, physical and mental."

In the relative world the soul experiences three different states: the waking state, the dream state, and the state of deep dreamless sleep. In the fourth state known as *turiya*, Atman is in its true nature as the detached witness of the soul's three states. During the state of deep sleep, the soul enjoys freedom from all sufferings and pains, but in turiya it experiences itself completely detached from all other states. Turiya, the superconscious state, is synonymous with samadhi. The difference between samadhi and deep sleep is seemingly very little. Deep sleep is a state of joy, but one is not aware of it. In samadhi the yogi is fully

aware of the blissful state. It is direct experience derived from Atman, but it cannot be fathomed through
any other means.

There are two types of samadhi: *savikalpa,* with
form; and *nirvikalpa,* without form. During savikalpa
samadhi the yogi looks at his own physical and mental states and processes as though they do not belong
to him. He remains completely detached. This is called
savikalpa samadhi because the thinker, the object, and
the means (thinking) are all present during this state.
In nirvikalpa samadhi one is free from all attachments.
In this deeper state, the means and objects of thought
do not exist; only the knower exists. Nirvikalpa is the
highest state in which the yogi merges with the bliss
eternal and remains in union with the real Self, the
Atman.

The experience of samadhi cannot be described,
for it is a unique state beyond thought, word, and
deed. Humans are bound by innumerable bondages.
When samadhi is achieved, the seeker is free forever.
This is the highest state, the permanent abode of
deathless yogis. Life after death can be experienced
here in this very life by those who have attained
samadhi, that state where the frontiers of death are
transcended.

The known part of life is a line that is stretched
between two points, birth and death. The vast portion of one's existence remains unknown and invis-
ible beyond these two known points. Ordinary mortals do not have any knowledge of the transition called
death, but the enlightened or accomplished yogis understand life here and hereafter. Those who have
learned to control the eleven gates know what is beyond, and that knowledge gives them mastery over
death as well as life.

Those who have gained this mastery are not

subject to the whims of death. They cast off their bodies and die under their own control at their own time. They consciously pass through the eleventh gate, through brahmarandhra. It is said that the one who travels through this gate knows about life hereafter exactly as he knows life here. There is no longer any veil between the two.

Accomplished yogis have learned to cast off the body in a variety of ways. We mention a few of the ancient techniques of yogis here only to make the point that there is another way to confront the act of dying besides the common one.

The general term for dying used by the yogis is *mahasamadhi*. Samadhi is the term for the highest state of tranquillity attainable by a human being. *Maha* means great. Yogis do not refer to the end of life as dying, but rather as casting off the body, letting go of what is no longer necessary—simple as that.

The technique of consciously letting go of the body was described to Nachiketa. Yama explained to him that of all the *nadis* or energy pathways in the body, the most important is *sushumna*. Sushumna passes upward through the center of the spinal column. Through sushumna flows the spiritual energy or divine force called *kundalini*. Sushumna is the key point of liberation. One who can enter sushumna at the time of death can attain Brahman, the highest goal of life. All other paths are paths of rebirths.

To leave the body, the yogi awakens the sleeping serpent power of kundalini and this energy enters into the path of sushumna. It rises to the *ajna chakra*, the two-petalled lotus between the eyebrows. Here the yogi gathers together and controls all the other life force energies of the body, known as the pranas. He withdraws his consciousness from earthbound existence and from the senses, and from the five lower chakras. He concentrates on the ajna chakra and then gradually upward toward *sahasrara,* the crown chakra. While concentrating on the crown of the head, he leaves the body through the fontanelle and rises finally to the realm of the absolute Brahman

One specific means of casting off the body is to freeze while in samadhi. This is a traditional way of dying for a particular group of Himalayan yogis. It is called *hima* samadhi. The yogi sits in samadhi in the stillness of the mountain cold and drops his freezing body.

Another similar technique is called *jala* samadhi. Performed inside the deep waters of the rivers of the Himalayas, the yogi retains his breath, and drops the body.

Sthala samadhi is done while sitting in the accomplished posture of yoga and consciously opening the brahmarandhra.

There is another very rare way of casting off the body. By meditating on the solar plexus the actual internal flame of fire within the body burns the body in a fraction of a second. Everything is reduced to ashes.

In all of these techniques, there is no pain. It is not like committing suicide which is an act of fear and despair. Yogis drop their bodies when those bodies no longer serve as proper instruments for enlightenment. When the body no longer serves one in the effort toward enlightenment, it is considered a burden. Such is the knowledge of life here and hereafter that was imparted from Yama to Nachiketa in the Kathopanishad.

I have personally witnessed yogis casting off the body consciously on many occasions. In the year 1938 when I was sent to Benares to stay with a Bengali couple, I was informed that the couple would drop their bodies at the same time. The couple had been meditating together for several years. They announced the date of their death and I was one of the witnesses.

I met a yogi at Paidung in Sikkim in the year 1947. Not only could he die at will, but he also could bring the dead back to life. During those days I was very anxious to know this mystery, termed *parakaya pravesha*. He demonstrated this feat in my presence five times. The yogi asked me to bring a living ant. I brought one, personally cut it with a sharp blade into three parts, and scattered them at a distance of ten feet. The yogi suddenly went into deep meditation. We examined his pulse, heartbeat, and breath, but there was no sign of life. Before he reached the state of deep meditation, there were violent jerks in his body.

The scattered parts of the ant moved together and united in a second's time. The ant came back to life and started crawling. We kept it under observation for three days. The yogi explained two methods of bringing the dead back to life — solar science and *pranavidya* (the science of prana). Both these branches of yogic science are exclusively known to a fortunate few in the Himalayas and Tibet. Jesus demonstrated his knowledge of these methods when he brought Lazarus back to life. Perhaps during his visit to Asia Minor he learned these techniques from the yogis.

Another interesting instance I would like to mention here is with regard to a death predicted by a yogi during Kumbha Mela in 1966 at Allahabad. One of my friends, Vinaya Maharaj, sent a messenger to my camp informing me that he was going to drop his body and I should come to witness it. On Vasanta Panchami (the celebration of the first day of spring) morning at 4:30 suddenly he said, "Now the time has come." Then he sat in the meditative posture, *siddhasana*, closed his eyes, and became silent. The sound 'tic' came from the cracking of the skull as he left his body through the brahmarandhra.

It is also possible for a highly advanced yogi to assume the dead body of another if he chooses to do so and if a suitable body is available. Only adepts know this technique. To the ordinary mind this seems like a fantasy.

The capacity to leave the body consciously at the time of death is not restricted only to accomplished yogis. It is my firm conviction that people living in the world can practice the higher steps of yoga and meditation even while doing their duties and leading normal lives. With sincere effort, proper preparation, and guidance, one who is not a yogi can also attain enlightenment before dropping the body.

Ramana Maharshi's mother was not an enlightened person though her son was. While she was dying, he placed one hand on her forehead and another on the heart region. Those who witnessed her death noticed that she went through agony for some time, but Ramana Maharshi's willpower helped her to cross the mire of delusion and she attained Self-realization.

I have witnessed two similar cases. One of these was in Minneapolis. The mother of a famous psychiatrist, Dr. Whitacre, had practised meditation for many years. At the time of death she went into deep samadhi and consciously dropped her body. The other was at Kanpur. There is a family of doctors there whose mother was a great devotee of the Lord. She was my initiate. Six months before her death, she decided to live in a room by herself remembering the Lord's name and meditating. After six months she fell sick and became bedridden. The time of her parting seemed imminent. During her last days she was completely detached and merged in her sadhana. She did not allow even her eldest son, Dr. A.N.Tandon, to remain in the room. Five minutes before her death she called all the family members and blessed them. Then she dropped her body in complete consciousness.

After her death, the walls of that room in which she lived vibrated with the sound of her mantra. Someone informed me of this and I could not believe it. So I visited the house and I discovered that the sound of her mantra was still vibrating there.

Mantra is a syllable or word or set of words. When the mantra is remembered consciously, it automatically is stored in the unconscious mind. At the time of parting, the mantra which is stored in the unconscious mind becomes one's guide. This period of separation is painful to the ignorant. This is not the case with a spiritual person who has remembered the mantra faithfully. The mantra serves as a guide through this period of transition. Mantra is a spiritual guide that dispels the fear of death and leads one fearlessly to the other shore of life.

For yogis and sages death is a minor event. To them it is merely a habit of the body, a change like other changes that occur in the process of growth. If everyone realized this, there would be less misery as people grow old and approach death. Death and birth are two gates of the same mansion. Coming out from one gate is called birth and passing through another gate is called death. Fortunate few know the mystery of birth and death.

Chapter Thirteen

Freedom from Attachment

Death is the critical moment of taking all the expe-
riences, thoughts, actions, memories, all that was spread
and diffused over one's life, and pushing it through a pin-
hole of time and space.

Casting off the body voluntarily and joyfully as
the yogis do is within the power of everyone, but not
many people will learn to do it. For most people, as
intriguing as mahasamadhi may be, those practices
are remote and seemingly unattainable. At the most,
these practices serve as a goal or as an inspiration
that life can be viewed differently from the ordinary,
and that death need not be something a person must
wait for and endure helplessly.

However, the fact is that mahasamadhi remains
out of the practical reach of most people. If it is true
that mahasamadhi is not practically attainable for the
average person, then how is death to be perceived?
Must death just be that dark mist that creeps into
everyone's existence whenever it pleases, snatching
people who are unwilling and unprepared, from their
lives? How can ordinary people be prepared for their
own deaths and for the deaths of those close to them?
How does a person diminish the sting of death, and
can people be truly comforted by the fact that death
is universal and certain?

As we have repeatedly stated, the fear of death stems from attachment. People are attached to their bodies and they identify with their bodies. The thought of the end of the body is understandably terrifying because that means the end to their assumed identity and existence. As long as we remain in ignorance and think that we are one with the body and its gross and subtle forms, we fear death and remain under the sway of death. The greatest obstacle in the path of realization is attachment to the body and to the objects of the world. This attachment makes us slaves. It is because of our attachments that we experience fear of death and loss. The more body-conscious and body-attached a person is, the greater the fear of dying.

The same principle applies to people who are attached to the things of the world, to their houses, property, clothing, jewelry, and money. They fear losing those things because they somehow offer meaning, identity, and worth. People also become very attached to other people. The emotion they feel for others gives them an identity and they fear giving up that identity in death. They fear the deaths of those to whom they are attached for similar reasons. If one's identity is somehow defined by attachment to others, the death of others then affects that identity.

The solution is to do away with these attachments to the body, property, possessions, and other people. This point cannot be made often enough. Reducing and finally eliminating attachments does not mean to escape life, to deny the enjoyment of life, or in any way to diminish life's value. Just the opposite occurs. Life is enhanced, enriched and expanded by reducing attachments. The person learns to love and give and open up to others and to the events of the world. Attachment means to grip, clasp, grasp, and hold on tightly. When death comes all that was being clutched and grasped is wrenched away. The tighter something is held, the greater will be the wrenching away, the deeper will be the pain. If life has been led with open hands, with no attachments, then death comes but there is nothing to be wrenched away.

We cannot all of a sudden wake one moment and let go of all attachments. It is a lifetime's work to undo the habit of forming attachments and requires attention every day, because the attractions and temptations of the world constantly work to strengthen attachments.

While spiritual seekers work on non-attachment, they must at the same time develop some understanding of what death is and what it does. Does death merely mean the end of life? Is it just this horrible event that comes without invitation, like some evil that crawls in the dark?

From an eastern metaphysical point of view, death cannot end life. The body stops and a person's moment in a particular blip of time and space ends. The individual does not end. From this perspective death does not appear dark and horrible. Death is as natural as birth, even as miraculous and beautiful as birth. Death, as well as birth, leads to life and growth.

In such a perspective, an individual enters a blip of time and space for a specific purpose and for a specific span of time. It is like plowing and sowing a field in the spring. The time and conditions are right to accomplish a purpose. The job must be done then. When the job is completed, there is no reason to remain in the field. Then it is time to wait, allow the seeds to sprout and the crops to grow. When the growing season is done, it is time to revisit the field — another purpose, another time.

That is the way human existence is. The world is like a field. An individual comes and prepares the field at the right time and goes away until it is the right time again to return and reap the harvest.

An individual's visit to worldly existence can be spoken of in terms of energy, or time and space, or karma, or a number of other philosophical notions. The philosophies declare that an individual has or is energy and that energy cannot be destroyed, only transmuted. The philosophies state that individuals enter specific time and space continuums and then leave them, moving onto others. They argue that an individual's karma drives his existence from one form to another, for certain experiences and for specific lengths of time. These philosophies can be useful and comforting. But regardless of all their understanding of philosophies, the idea of death looms in all people and sometimes all the readings of the world's philosophies cease to be effective. Death remains an event we must face alone. Only our own philosophy—that which we have personally realized—matters at the time of death.

Death is an individual's confrontation with the most fundamental fear. Whatever self-transforming work a person does in life, no matter what forms her or his philosophy takes, the imagining of the moment of death is frightening. To some degree all people experience fear of dying. We can tell ourselves with varying degrees of certainty that death is not so scary. We can say it is merely a change from one state of existence or awareness to another. We can say that at least death means an end to the pain of life, or perhaps it is a gateway to an everlasting life. Whatever we comfort ourselves with, there are still bubbles of fear present. We fear death. That fear, great or small, becomes more intense and focused at the actual moment of departure from this world. All philosophies are set aside as this fear becomes real.

But this natural fear can also potentially be of great benefit. It draws the dying person's attention and concentrates it. How and upon what a dying person focuses reflects the contents of the life just lived and sets in motion the life to be lived next.

Death is the critical moment of taking all the experiences, thoughts, actions, memories, all that was spread and diffused over one's life, cramming it into a single dot, a single moment, and pushing it through a pinhole of time and space. The energy employed in the thrust of that momentum and all that is with it, and pushing it through is enormous. It is sufficient to shape another life.

How we come to that pinhole, what we bring to it, and how we pass through it, are queries of tremendous importance. How life is lived, the journey that takes a person to death, are matters of immense significance.

The comparison is often made between sleeping and dying. How a day is spent determines the quality of sleep that night. If a person goes to bed full of regrets, fears, and the feeling of being unfulfilled and discontent, sleep will be fitful and all those negative thoughts will be carried into the next day, largely determining the quality of that day. Unfulfilled desires of one day will penetrate into the next day and affect that day's mental and emotional tone. The new day is in effect stolen from the sort of sleep that ended the previous day.

Go into sleep free and contented so the next day can be embraced fully and its value and purpose can best be attained and appreciated. Do your best with the day at hand, and let go. Tomorrow will take care of itself. Each day has its own value and its own purpose.

The same phenomenon occurs in death. The

quality of life to the moment of death largely determines the state of mind of the dying person. In death the mind becomes very focused. It is a moment of true meditation, of very solid one-pointedness. If a person's life has been characterized by fear and dread, then those qualities will be magnified at the time of death. If a person has led an undisciplined life, then death will come in a similarly undisciplined way.

Death is beyond the control of a person who has led his life without purpose or discipline. If a person has not controlled the body or the mind, nor channeled the urges for food, sleep and sex, then the moment of death will be beyond his control. All the unfulfilled desires, all the fears, and all the tendencies to want to satisfy one's urges willfully abound at the time of death, as undisciplined as they were throughout life. Whatever follows in that person's existence will be determined by that internal commotion, just as the restless, anxiety-ridden sleep of the night determines the quality of the following day.

However, the person who has led a disciplined life and has learned to let go of attachments, can pass gracefully from this life and into the next. This person can leave like a guest who knows the visit is over. Her purpose of life has been accomplished. With an exhalation she departs. She simply goes, knowing that the reality is within, eternal, unaffected by, and independent of the people and things of the world that must be left behind.

In India it is the tradition to remind others and oneself that when a soul's moment has come to depart this world, let it depart. That soul no longer belongs in this time and space. Let it go.

At the time of death in India the second chapter of the Bhagavad Gita is read as a reminder to be both fearless in the face of death, and to contemplate the journey of the soul. At the start of the second chapter, Arjuna is faced with the prospect of death. He is afraid, grieving, and depressed. His teacher, Krishna, tells him not to be afraid, not to fall into weakness, but to arise like fire. "Why all this emotion because of death?" Krishna asks him. Life and death are part of the same turning wheel, each one half of the circle, each moving and turning with and toward the other.

Chapter Fourteen

Who am I?

Atman must be reached, penetrated, and known by experience.

An old story of creation narrates that after the heavens, all the stars, the earth, the air, the waters, the sky, and all the creatures on land and in the sea were made, God created humankind. When the first human awoke and became conscious of worldly life for the first time, he looked around at the lakes and rivers, the mountains and forests, at the leaping fish, the flying birds, and the great herds of animals. He was silent. He looked to the heavens and the sun and moon and the great blackness of space with its millions of stars. He was silent. He looked then at God. He was silent. When he had taken in everything around him, including the Lord himself, this first human on earth looked finally at himself and said, "Who am I?"

This first human did not look at the animals or stars and say, "What are they?" He did not ask, "Where am I?" He did not even ask of God, "Who are you?" His first words, his first wondering thoughts and first curiosity were to know his own identity.

That is the question that drives all human beings. Everything a human being does and wants involves that question. People want happiness and peace. Instinctively they know that the acquisition of happiness and peace rests with the answer to the question, "Who am I?"

To consciously realize this as the question of life is the first big step on a sacred journey. The next big step is to find the answer.

Nachiketa of the Kathopanishad knew that the answer lay hidden in the great circle of life and death and demanded that Yama explain its mystery. Nachiketa had the strength, patience, and perseverance necessary not to take Yama's no for an answer, nor to take anything less than knowledge as the boon.

Atman is the answer. I am Atman. You are Atman. I and you are One. That is the answer.

As Yama told Nachiketa, it is not enough to hear of Atman. Atman must be reached, penetrated, and known by experience. Yama explained that learning does not suffice to reach Atman, nor does simply the use of the intellect, nor sacred teaching.

To reach Atman requires choice and action.

That is the message of the Kathopanishad and the meaning of life and death. Nachiketa was given a choice. He was offered all the greatest things there are in worldly life — wealth, power, sensual pleasures. He chose otherwise. To have chosen worldly attractions would have meant another round in the endless cycle of death and birth. In each attraction there would be a flash of pleasure, followed by a stream of pain, followed by fear of loss, and finally death. Each worldly thing would change and die. People feel the pain from these attractions, but nonetheless they continue to believe that these things will next time, ultimately, bring peace and happiness. This belief, as Nachiketa knew, brings people back to the plane of attractions again and again, to live, desire, fear, and then die again.

The Kathopanishad says, "The foolish run after outward pleasures and fall into the snares of vast-embracing death."

The old God of Deuteronomy in the Bible says plainly:

"I have set before you life and death, a blessing and a curse. Therefore choose life."

Choose what does not die. That's the solution to the mystery. Atman is the answer. The challenge is to find Atman.

The things of the world are meant to be enjoyed. It is unwise to be attached to them because they do not last. Enjoy the things of the world, then let them go. Let them pass through your life. Embrace all of life, take in all of life, but do it with wisdom and move toward knowledge. Worldly life is a means, not an end.

To live life well is an art. It requires not only wisdom but courage. "This bondage of the human being to a non-eternal reality," said Shankara, "cannot be broken by weapons, or by wind, or fire, or by millions of acts. Nothing but the sharp sword of knowledge can cut through this bondage. It is forged by discrimination and made keen by purity of heart, through divine grace."

Life is brief and precious. Don't waste your time here in the rat's cage of objects and temptations. Don't run after pleasures. Use the things of the world for spiritual growth. That is choosing life.

The goal is Atman. The message of the Upanishads is that there is only One. All is One. Having desires for the things of the world translates the One into many. Yama told Nachiketa, "Who sees the many and not the One, wanders on from death to death."

The choice is God or mammon, permanent or transitory, many, Atman, or the desires of the world. One means life and the other death. That is the mystery.

Swami Rama

Swami Rama was born in the Himalayas and was initiated by his master into many yogic practices. He was sent by his master to other yogis and adepts of the Himalayas to gain new perspectives and insights into the ancient teachings. At the young age of twenty-four he was installed as Shankaracharya of Karvirpitham in South India. Swamiji relinquished this position to pursue intense sadhana in the caves of the Himalayas. Having successfully completed this sadhana, he was directed by his master to go to Japan and to the West In order to illustrate the scientific basis of the ancient yogic practices. At the Menninger Foundation in Topeka, Kansas, Swamiji convincingly demonstrated the capacity of the mind to control so-called involuntary physiological processes such as the heart rate, temperature, and brain waves. Swamiji's work in the United States continued for twenty-three years, and in this period he established the Himalayan International Institute.

Swamiji became well known in the United States as a yogi, teacher, philosopher, poet, humanist, and philanthropist. His models of preventive medicine, holistic health, and stress management have permeated the mainstream of western mediicne. In 1993 Swamiji returned to India where he established the Himalayan Institute Hospital Trust in the foothills of the Garhwal Himalayas. Swamiji left this physical plane in November, 1996, but the seeds he has sown continue to sprout, bloom , and bear fruit. His teachings, embodied in the words, "Love, Serve, Remember," continue to inspire the many students whose good fortune it was to come in contact with such an accomplished, selfless, and loving master.

Himalayan Institute
Hospital Trust

Perhaps the most visible form of Swami Rama's service to humanity is the Himalayan Institute Hospital Trust (HIHT). HIHT is a nonprofit organization committed to the premise that all human beings have the right to health, education, and economic self-sufficiency. The comprehensive health care and social development programs of HIHT incorporate medical care, education, and research. The philosophy of HIHT is: love, serve, and remember.

The mission of the Trust is to develop integrated and cost-effective approaches to health care and development that address the local population, and which can serve as a model for the country as a whole, and for the underserved population worldwide. A combined approach in which traditional systems of health care complement modern medicine and advanced technology is the prime focus of clinical care, medical education, and research at HIHT.

HIHT is located in the newly formed state of Uttaranchal, one of the underdeveloped states of India. A bold vision to bring medical services to the millions of people in northern India, many of whom are underprivileged and have little or no health care, began modestly in 1989 with a small outpatient department. Today it is the site of a world class medical city and educational campus that includes: a large state-of-the-art hospital offering a full range of medical specialities and services, a holistic health program, a medical college, a school of nursing, a rural development institute, and accommodations for staff, students, and patients' families. This transformation is the result of the vision of Sri Swami Rama.

For information contact:
Himalayan Institute Hospital Trust
Swami Rama Nagar, P.O. Doiwala
Distt. Dehradun 248140, Uttaranchal, India
Tel:91-135-412068, Fax:91-135-412008
hihtsrc@sancharnet.in; www.hihtindia.org

Conscious Living
A Guidebook for Spiritual Transformation
Swami Rama

This is a practical book for people living in the world. The word "practical" implies that the teaching can be practiced in the world, in the midst of family, career and social obligations. No prior preparation is required for reading this book, and after reading this book, no further teaching is required. If one were to sincerely practice the teachings presented by Sri Swami Rama in this book, one will surely achieve the goal of self-realization, a state described by Swamiji as the summum bonum of life, a state of bliss, a state of perfection.

ISBN 8-188157-03-1; $12.95, paperback, 160 pages

Let the Bud of Life Bloom
A Guide to Raising Happy and Healthy Children
Swami Rama

"Childhood is pure. If we impart good education to our children, become selfless examples for them, and give them love, perhaps they will grow and become the best citizens of the world. Then, the whole universe will bloom like a flower."

In *Let the Bud of Life Bloom*, Swami Rama gives us relevant, practical insights into forming the basis of a happy life through a happy childhood. Through blending the best of our ancient values with new inventions, children can grow into healthy, creative adults.

ISBN 8-188157-04-X; $12.95, paperback, 100 pages

Available from your local bookseller or: To order send price of book plus $2.50 for 1st book and .75 for each additional book (within US) (Wi. res. add 5.5% sales tax) to: Lotus Press, PO Box 325, Twin Lakes, WI 53181, USA; Toll Free: 800-824-6396 Phone: 1-262-889-8561; Fax: 1-262-889-2461 lotuspress@lotuspress.com; www.lotuspress.com